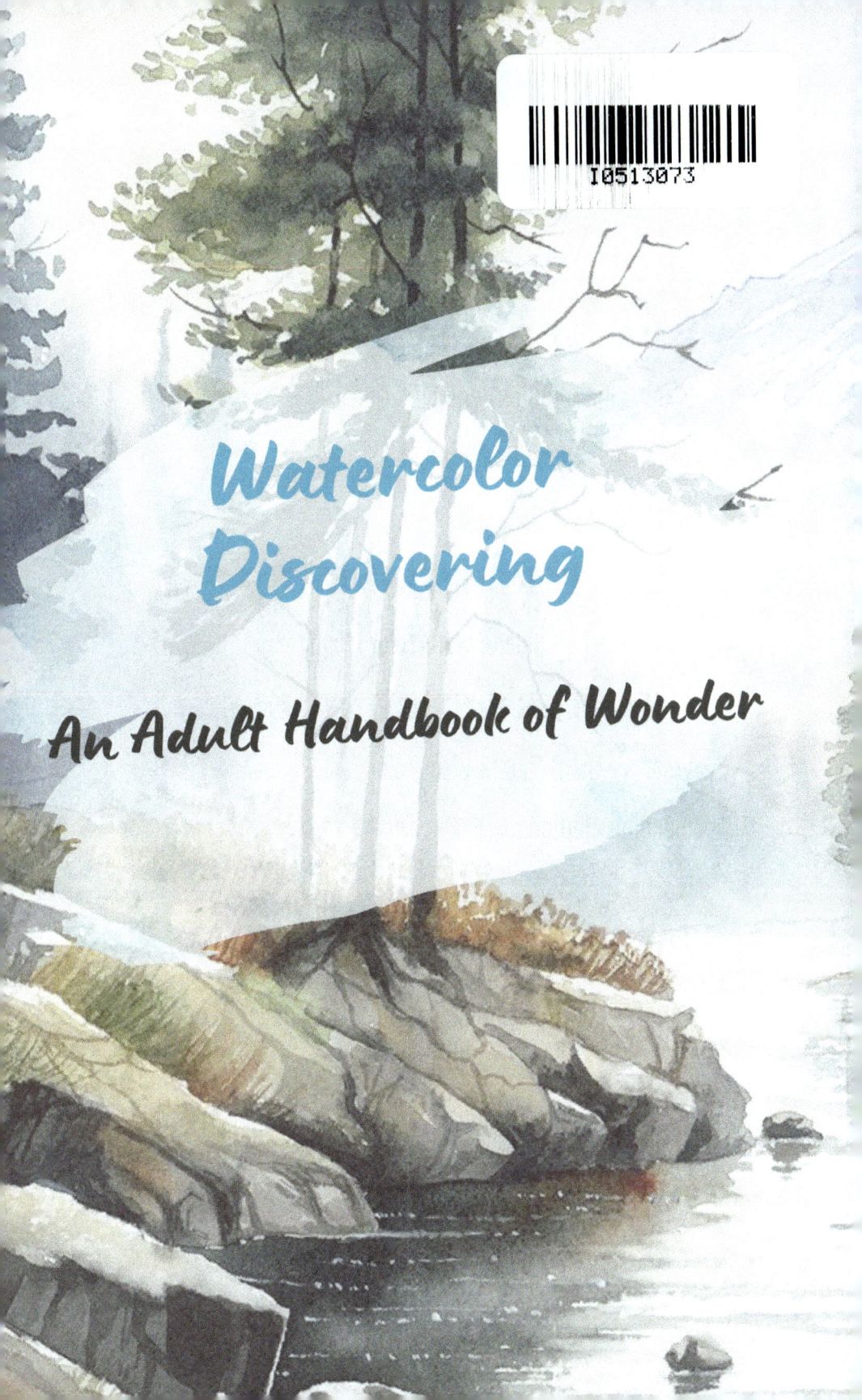

Watercolor Discovering

An Adult Handbook of Wonder

Table of contents

INTRODUCTION — 1

CHAPTER 1: MATERIALS
Watercolor Supplies Beginners Guide — 3
Watercolor Terms and Vocabulary — 29
Water Control — 34

CHAPTER 2: MIXING
The Essential Guide to Watercolor Mixing — 36

CHAPTER 3: TECHNIQUES
What are the Different Watercolor Techniques? — 49
Blending Methods — 54
Washes — 55

CHAPTER 4: THE 3 PROJECTS
Easy Watercolor Painting Tutorial for Beginners — 58
A Step-By-Step Watercolor Landscape Tutorial — 67
Lovely Loose Watercolor Flowers Tutorial — 77

INTRODUCTION

Greetings from the world of watercolors! Have you ever found yourself enthralled by the delicate strokes and brilliant hues of a watercolor painting? Maybe you've always wanted to try it because you've appreciated how expressive the medium is. Well, there's no need to search any farther! This beginner's workbook is intended especially for individuals like you who are interested in learning more about the wonder of watercolor painting. We recognize that embarking on a fresh creative endeavor might be scary. So do not panic! Your confidence will grow with each project as you follow the step-by-step instructions in this workbook, which will help you understand even the most fundamental skills.

Here's what to anticipate:
* Simple directions: No prior artistic knowledge is required. Every lesson simplifies complex processes into doable stages so that you can start producing stunning artwork right away.
* Put enjoyment first: We think education should be pleasurable. This workbook is jam-packed with fun projects that will keep you inspired and eager to watch how your abilities advance.
* Perfectionism is attained through practice: With guided exercises and sample room for experimentation, you'll have what you need to refine your watercolor techniques and find your own style.

Let your imagination run wild and enjoy the delightful mishaps that watercolor painting presents. You are welcome to unwind, explore, and paint your way to creative satisfaction. Now let's get started!

Chapter 1: Materials

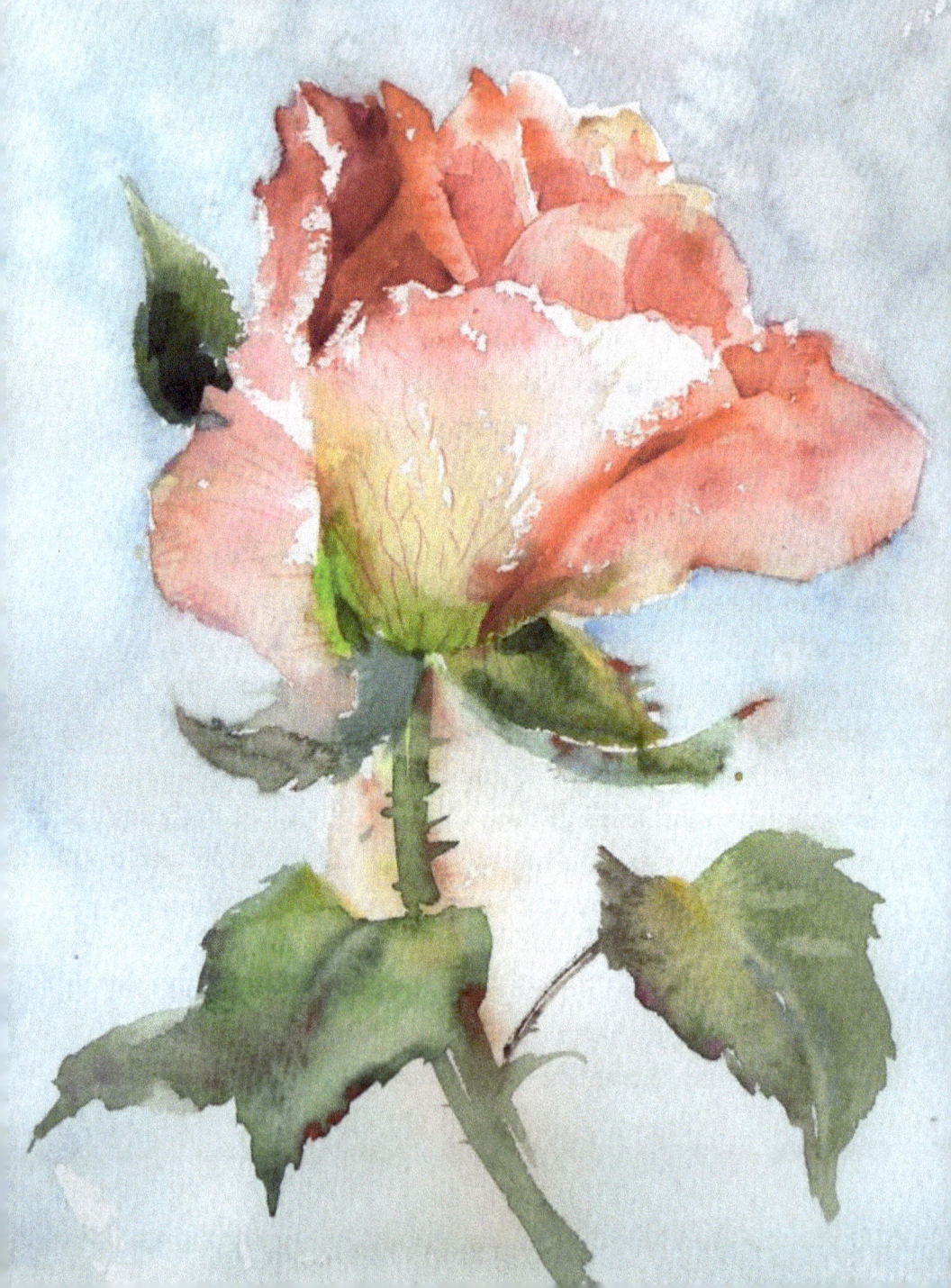

Watercolor Supplies Beginners Guide (This is What you Truly Need)

Of course, the fundamentals are paint, paper, and brushes. All of these are available in a wide range of qualities and prices. Beyond that you also need a few other bits of equipment for happy painting.

For me, the **minimum list** of supplies is as follows:
- **Paint**
- **Paper**
- **Brushes**
- **A palette (for mixing and/or storing paints)**
- **Water jars**
- **A flat board**
- **Masking tape & masking fluid**
- **Cloth or absorbent paper towels**

Let's have a look at each of these in detail and I'll give you my recommendations on the best alternatives for each.

Watercolor Supplies Beginners Guide (This is What you Truly Need)

Best Watercolor Paints to get Started

- Why purchase cheaper lower quality paint which you'll end up abandoning in favor of artist quality paints as your skills progress. To me it seems like a false economy, especially since a few tubes of watercolor paint can last for months or even years.

- Also, If you're not sure you'll enjoy watercolors you only need a small amount of paint. Why buy big tubes of student grade paint when you can get a kit of small artist grade paints for the same price and get the full quality experience of watercolors.

- I say this because student grade paints may be cheaper, but they also have a lower pigment load than artist grade paints. This means the final appearance will be less vibrant than what can be achieved with artist grade watercolors.

- For this reason I recommend you start out with a small selection of artist quality paints, which I'll talk about below.

Watercolor Supplies Beginners Guide (This is What you Truly Need)

How many colors do you need for watercolor?

In my opinion you only need a few paints to be able to mix a wide range of different colors. For me the basis of any watercolor palette is a warm and cool version of each primary color. These will allow you to mix a good range of colors including bright saturated hues and neutral darker tints as necessary.

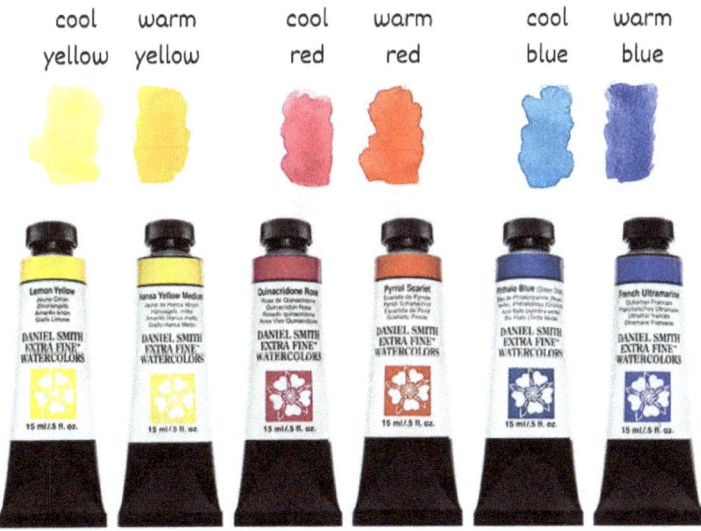

Why warm and cool primaries? The color appearance of paints is dictated by the pigments used in their ingredients. These can be classified into "warm" (the pigments have a touch of red, orange or yellow) or "cool" (they tend towards greens, blues and violets). Depending on whether you mix warm or cool colors together you get different results!

Watercolor Supplies Beginners Guide (This is What you Truly Need)

Having both warm and cool primaries provides a wider range of mixing possibilities.

Here's an example of the range of colors you can produce with just these six paints, and this is just a small example of what you can achieve:

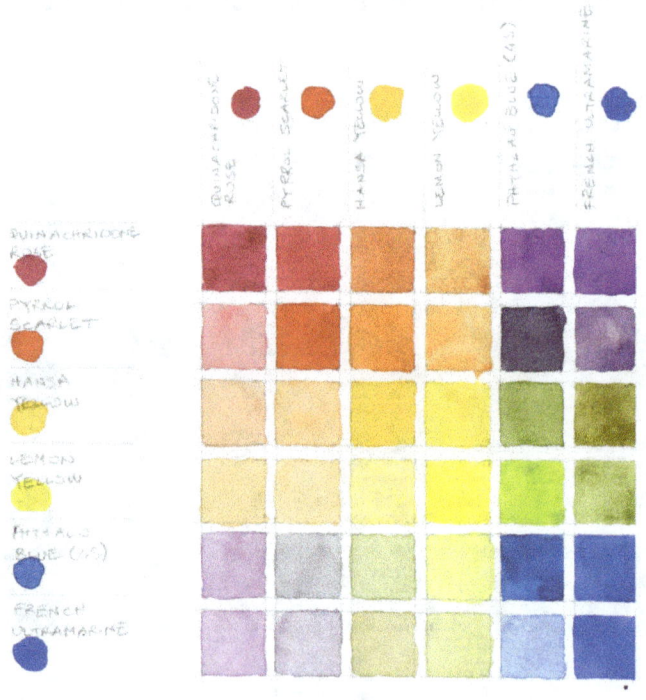

Tips & Tricks: Paint names vary from one brand to another but pigment numbers are universal. Like this you can use the pigment numbers to find equivalent paint colors by other manufacturers if you prefer. You can buy each of these individually but you'll get a better deal if you buy a set of small tubes

Watercolor Supplies Beginners Guide (This is What you Truly Need)

What about black and white watercolor paint?

Note that you don't need black and you don't want to use white watercolor either. Black can be mixed using other colors, and the color white comes from the paper itself (you just don't paint the paper in the places you want to see white).

Admittedly, sometimes you need to add some white highlights back into a piece of artwork. But you don't use white watercolor for this. The best solution is white gouache like this:

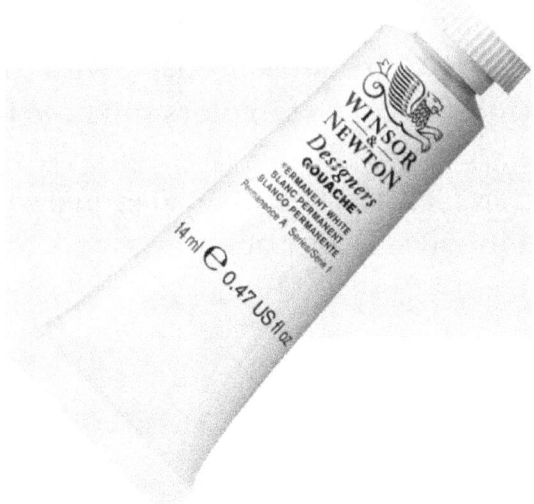

Unlike watercolor, gouache is opaque and will hide the underlying color so you can add white back to a watercolor painting.

Watercolor Supplies Beginners Guide (This is What you Truly Need)

Beginners Watercolor Brushes

Brushes are an extension of your hand. They help translate your intentions onto paper. As such they are one of the most important parts of your painting equipment.

I've lost count of how many brushes I've purchased over the years, but you only really need two or three brushes to get started. You can always expand your collection later.

Do you need special brushes for watercolor?
- When you paint with watercolors you wouldn't use the same brushes as an oil painter or acrylic artist.
- The brushes used in watercolor painting have been specially designed to handle properly with this medium. To get the most out of watercolors you need to choose wisely.
- Not all watercolor brushes are made equal so you still need to know what to look out for.

Watercolor Supplies Beginners Guide (This is What you Truly Need)

What type of brush is best for watercolor?

It's commonly accepted that the best kind of brush for watercolor painting uses natural hair.

Sable is very much appreciated for its ability to hold water and the springiness of the hairs (this helps to form a good tip).

Squirrel hair has also been used by watercolor artists for generations because of its huge water holding capacity.

Brushes for watercolor are generally available in **three main types** of hair:
- **Natural hair**
- **Synthetic fibers**
- **Blended hairs** (a mixture of natural and synthetic)

Personally I wouldn't recommend using synthetic fibers. Of all the alternatives these have the lowest water holding ability. I prefer natural hair or a blended mix which provides a good compromise at a cheaper price.

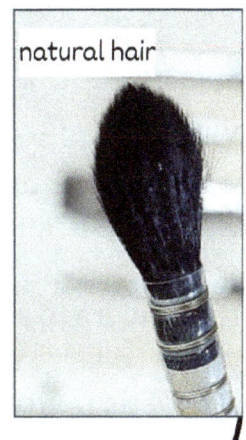

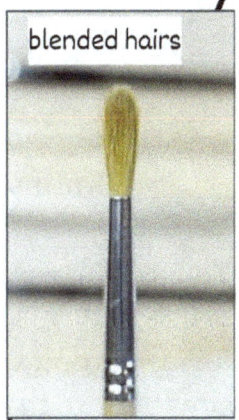

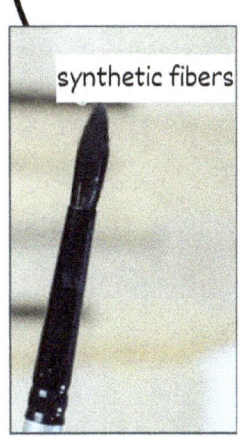

Watercolor Supplies Beginners Guide (This is What you Truly Need)

How many watercolor brushes do I need?

You can easily do any type of watercolor painting techniques with a minimum of three brushes. A large round brush, a wash brush, and a small round brush.

If you were to start with just one brush I would recommend you get a large round brush made of sable or some kind of synthetic mixture designed to simulate the characteristics of sable.

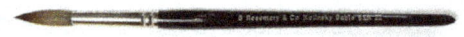

Kolinsky Sable series 22 size 8 (short handle)

You could easily do the majority of your painting with a brush like this. It's a perfect size (not too big or too small), it forms a good tip and has a good "spring" (in other words it goes back to its original form).

A cheaper alternative which uses a blend of sable and synthetic is this designer brush, also by Rosemary & Co:

Rosemary & Co Sable Blend Series 402 – Size 12 (short handle)

Watercolor Supplies Beginners Guide (This is What you Truly Need)

How many watercolor brushes do I need?

The next most important kind of brush is a **"wash" brush**. This is used for painting big areas of color, such as when painting skies or backgrounds. Wash brushes include:
- **Flat brushes** (the wide flat edge lets you cover a lot of surface with each brush stroke)
- **Mop brushes** (these bushes have a big head and a large water holding capacity).

One of my favorite wash brushes is this squirrel hair mop by **Da Vinci:**

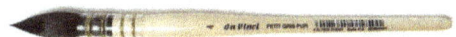

Da Vinci Blue Squirrel mop series 418 size 4

Squirrel hair is not as "springy" as sable, so the brush head deforms slightly when you paint but it holds a ton of water and handles beautifully. A lot of artists who prefer a loose style of painting only use squirrel hair.

You could also go with a less expensive synthetic alternative such as this:

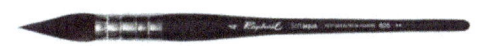

Raphaël Soft Aqua series 805 size 4

Watercolor Supplies Beginners Guide (This is What you Truly Need)

Watercolor Paper

Choosing watercolor paper is a bit of a dilemma.

You only get the best results from artist quality paper. But good quality paper is expensive! Student grade paper simply doesn't handle the same way with watercolor paints, making it more of a struggle to control your painting process.

Student grade paper simply won't show you all the beautiful characteristics of watercolors...

Sorry!

What paper is best for watercolor?
- It's important to know what to look for so you can make an informed choice.
- The best type of watercolor paper is **100% cotton, pH neutral and acid free.**
- Neutral, acid free paper is known as **"archival quality"** because it won't affect the paint and doesn't fade over time. Cotton is naturally white so it doesn't need any chemical treatment. Cotton is also naturally absorbent, softer, and stronger than wood-based paper.
- One of the best artist quality papers, and the one that I use the most is the brand **Arches**

Watercolor Supplies Beginners Guide (This is What you Truly Need)

Watercolor Paper

Other types of finish exist such as hot-press paper which you can read more about here.

I think you need to experience both high quality and student quality paper to know the capabilities of each. Like that you will understand the way the paint behaves is a result of the material you're using and not a reflection of your skills.

Cotton paper is usually the best choice for the best painting experience, but watercolor papers are also available as a mixture of cotton and wood fibers or wood-based only.

For example, an interesting compromise is watercolor paper made from 50% cotton and 50% wood cellulose. They are slightly cheaper and they represent some of the advantages of 100% cotton with less of the problems of 0% wood-only papers. The brand Paul Rubens make a good value paper like this:

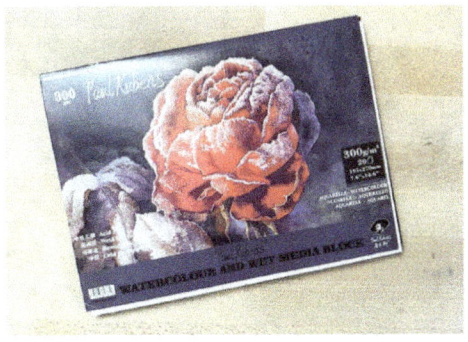

Paul Rubens watercolor block 50% cotton rag

Watercolor Supplies Beginners Guide (This is What you Truly Need)

Watercolor Paper

Watercolors are a lot of fun and you can easily use up paper doing sketches and experiments. For this kind of use I recommend you use lower quality paper.

Using low quality paper is more of a challenge, but you simply have to accept the shortcomings of student grade paper, and above all remember that you can probably achieve better results when you use artist grade.

Canson XL is a student grade paper which I use frequently. It has a good thickness for water-based uses and handles pretty well. For better value I buy bigger pads and cut down the sheets to a smaller size:

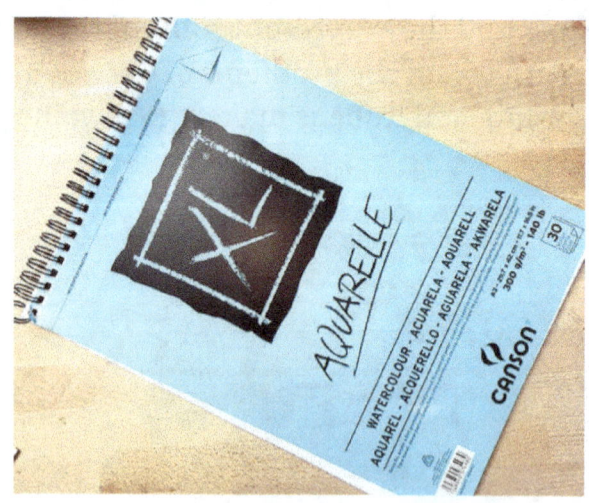

Canson XL watercolor pad 140 lb / 300 gsm

Watercolor Supplies Beginners Guide (This is What you Truly Need)

Watercolor Paper

One last recommendation for those of you looking for cheap 100% cotton paper. Arteza is a Florida based company who aims to offer affordable art supplies to budding artists.

They have a great deal for a double pack of watercolor pads. I've tested this paper and it performs quite well. Wet-on-wet dispersion is good and you can blend smoothly. But paint lifts too easily when re-wetting colored washes which can make glazing and layering paint tricky. Also the texture of the paper is a bit flat for my liking.

After testing I would consider this a decent student quality paper for watercolor artists:

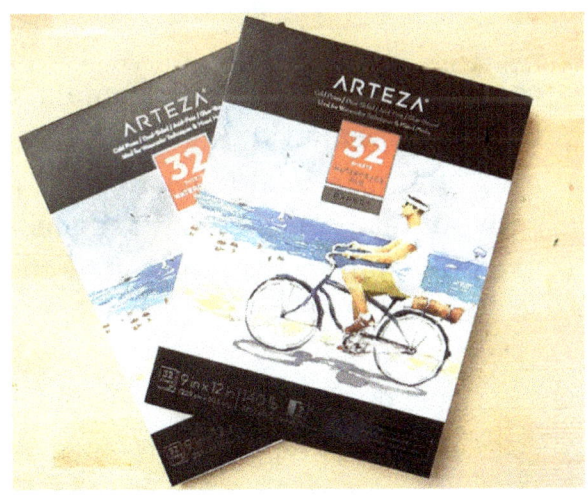

Arteza 100% cotton 140 lb 300gsm Expert watercolor pad

Watercolor Supplies Beginners Guide (This is What you Truly Need)

Watercolor Palettes

There are a few different types of palettes used by watercolorists, and again the variety of choice can be pretty confusing. I would categorize palettes into a few different types:
- **Studio paint palettes**
- **Portable paint palettes**
- **Mixing palettes**

Let me explain.

A studio paint palette is the kind of thing you use exclusively indoors. It would contain a number of empty wells for squeezing out paint plus a surface for mixing colors. They can range in size.

A portable paint palette takes the form of a metal or plastic box with a folding lid. It's small and compact enough for traveling, painting outdoors, or studio painting. You can fill the box with "pans" of ready-made paint or squeeze paint from a tube into empty pans to customize your choice of colors.

A mixing palette is used purely for mixing up paints and has no wells for storing paint colors.

Watercolor Supplies Beginners Guide (This is What you Truly Need)

Watercolor Palettes

How do I choose a watercolor palette?

A good palette should have a bright white surface to help you clearly see the colors that you're mixing. The size of the paint wells should also fit the size of brush you use the most. Bigger wells are more comfortable for picking up paint with a large brush.

The material should also be resistant and easy to clean.

Also, think about how you're going to use your palette. Do you have a fixed place to paint indoors where you can leave your equipment and come back to paint when you like?

I work mostly indoors in my studio. My absolute favorite palette is the John Pike palette(named after a well known artist from the 1960's). I love it for several reasons. It has a big mixing surface for mixing colors. The wells are big enough to take a large brush without getting color contamination from one well to another. And it has a lid which protects the paints from dust while not in use.

Watercolor Supplies Beginners Guide (This is What you Truly Need)

Watercolor Palettes

Original John Pike 20 well watercolor palette

Are you going to be moving around a lot to do your painting? Whether you like to paint outdoors on the move or you just need to pack away your paints neatly, a folding box palette would suit you well.

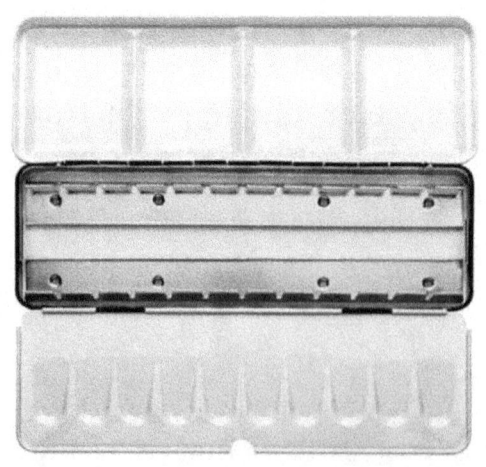

Empty Watercolor Tin, 24 Pan

Watercolor Supplies Beginners Guide (This is What you Truly Need)

Watercolor Palettes

Some palettes lack room for mixing colors so artists use an additional mixing palette simply to have more room. A couple of extra mixing palettes I like to use include porcelain palettes like this and enameled butchers trays. The advantage of both porcelain and enamel is that they are both stain resistant, unlike plastic alternatives.

But keep in mind you can also just use a plate ! (if you do, try to use a white porcelain plate – ceramic tends to stain. Also you should reserve the plate only for watercolors to avoid any potential paint toxicity problems)

Watercolor Supplies Beginners Guide (This is What you Truly Need)

Other Must Have Watercolor Supplies

There's a whole bunch of other equipment you can find for painting, but among the most important for watercolor artists is the following. These are the things I have started to use on a regular basis because they are the best adapted to the painting process with watercolors.

A flat board

I hardly ever do a watercolor without fixing down the paper onto a flat board. This has multiple advantages including helping to keep the paper flat, allowing you to tilt the board when working with wet paint, and being able to rotate the sheet to make brush work easier in difficult positions.

I use wooden boards without any kind of surface treatment. They will stain, but frankly that doesn't matter. I've tried boards with varnishes before and they can react badly when you do a lot of wet-on-wet painting (one time, the varnish stuck to the underside of the paper!)

A drawing board (get a simple wooden board like this)

Watercolor Supplies Beginners Guide (This is What you Truly Need)

Other Must Have Watercolor Supplies

Gummed tape

While we're on the subject of tape, the "gummed" variety is used by watercolor artists to help fix down paper during the stretching process. This stuff reminds me of the envelopes you have to lick to get them to stick ! Yuk !

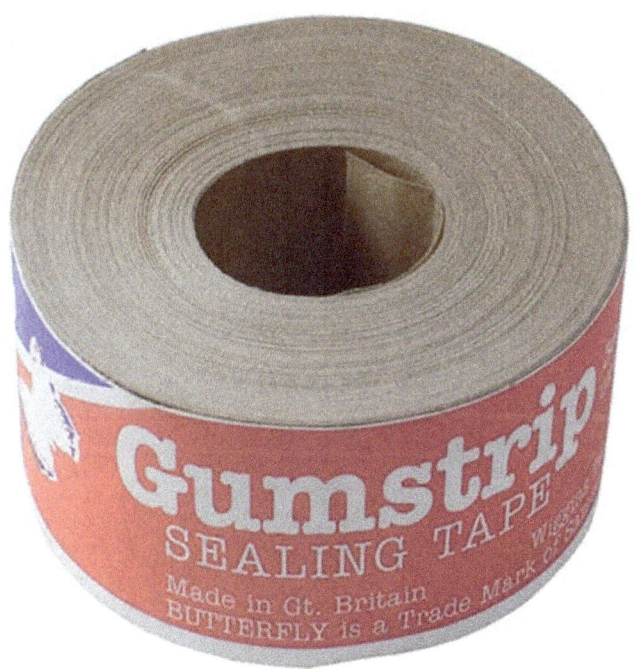

Get some gummed tape (for stretching paper)

Watercolor Supplies Beginners Guide (This is What you Truly Need)

Other Must Have Watercolor Supplies

Mason Jars

You need something big to hold a decent amount of water for mixing colors and rinsing brushes. I find mason jars are the perfect size. Also glass is an inert material which stains less over time.

The trick is to use two jars when painting. One is for rinsing and the other is to have a supply of clean water for making fresh mixtures and adding clear water to paper when needed (wet-on-wet techniques).

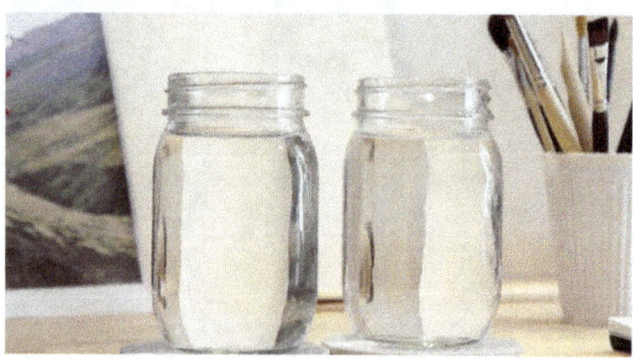

Mason jars (16oz glass jars like this are the perfect size)

Watercolor Supplies Beginners Guide (This is What you Truly Need)

Other Must Have Watercolor Supplies

Liquid masking fluid

When you paint with watercolors you'll find you need some kind of liquid masking. Most of the time the color white comes from the underlying paper. But there are many occasions when it becomes impractical to paint around small white shapes. It can make you lose time and potentially ruin a painting. I recently changed the brand of masking fluid I was using for an odorless version (a much better option, especially if you're sensitive to strong chemical smells).

There are a number of different ways to make use of masking fluid – this article should help

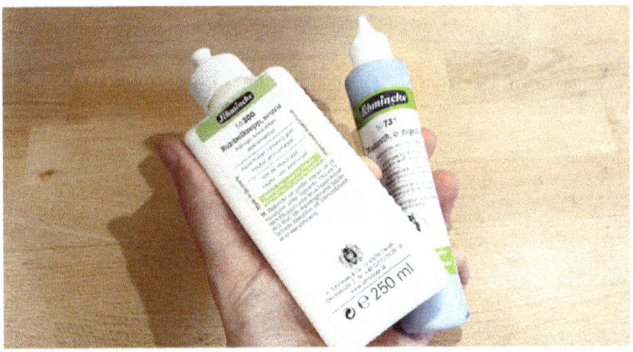

Liquid frisket or masking fluid (get an odorless version like this one)

Watercolor Supplies Beginners Guide (This is What you Truly Need)

Other Must Have Watercolor Supplies

White gouache

Sometimes you forget to leave a highlight in a painting or you have a lot of white details to add back to a finished watercolor. I always have a tube of artists white gouache handy for this kind of thing. Gouache paint is also water based but it's opaque so you can cover up the underlying color.

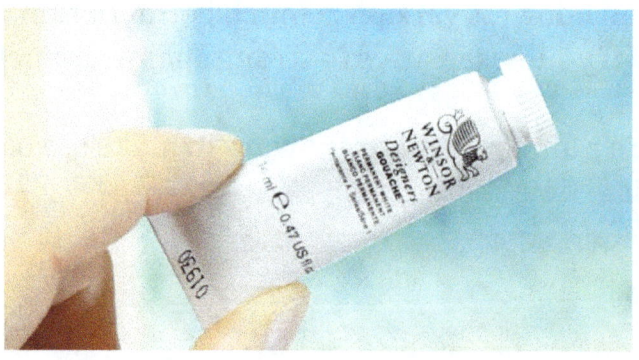

White gouache (I like Winsor & Newton permanent white)

Watercolor Supplies Beginners Guide (This is What you Truly Need)

Other Must Have Watercolor Supplies

Pipettes

Very cheap and very practical, I use pipettes like this every time I paint to transfer clear water from the jar to the mixing palette. I use them to add a few drops of water to the wells of dry paint so that the colors reactivate. I also use them to add a big puddle of water to the mixing surface when I need to mix up a good amount of color.

Spray bottle (or "spritzer" if you prefer)

A spray bottle

Very cheap and very practical, I use pipettes like this every time I paint to transfer clear water from the jar to the mixing palette. I use them to add a few drops of water to the wells of dry paint so that the colors reactivate. I also use them to add a big puddle of water to the mixing surface when I need to mix up a good amount of color.

Watercolor Supplies Beginners Guide (This is What you Truly Need)

Other Must Have Watercolor Supplies

A *few* pencils

Be careful not to use pencils which are too hard on watercolor paper because they can leave indentations in the surface after you erase them. The hardest pencil I use is a HB, and on watercolor paper I tend to use nothing softer than 2B. I do use much softer pencils as well when sketching and doing value studies. Staedtler Lumograph is one of my favorite brands…

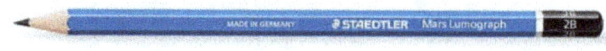

Pencils (this is my preferred brand)

**A *kneaded eraser*015

I wonder who invented these things. I think they're great ! A kneaded eraser is a bit like a lump of putty which you can mold into any shape you like for erasing. On top of that they do not leave any residue on the surface of the paper, unlike traditional erasers !

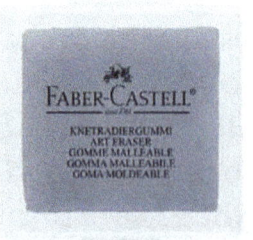

Get a kneaded eraser (you'll wonder why you never tried them)

Watercolor Supplies Beginners Guide (This is What you Truly Need)

Other Must Have Watercolor Supplies

A watercolor sketchbook

Sketchbooks are a good habit to start. I find they help you to practice regularly without the fear of doing a "finished" piece of art. I like the Stillman & Birn beta series. The paper is bright white and has a smooth finish which is good for both pencil sketching and watercolor painting. And the paper is thick enough to handle the wetness without much warping.

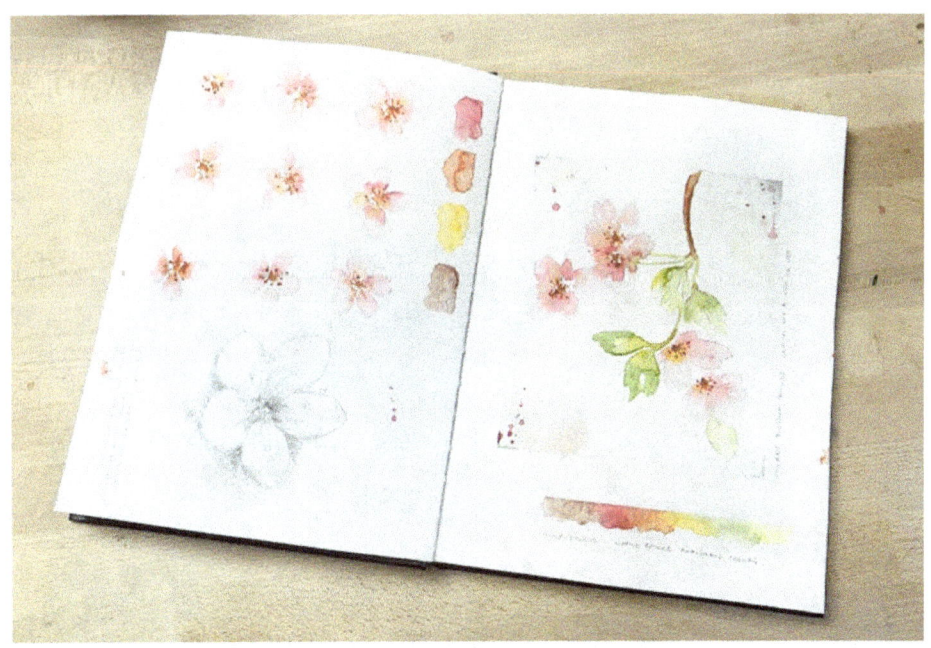

Sketchbook (get one like this which can handle wet media)

Watercolor Supplies Beginners Guide (This is What you Truly Need)

Other Must Have Watercolor Supplies

Absorbent cloths

An absorbent cloth of some kind is another essential bit of kit. You use these to blot your brush to help vary the wetness of your brush strokes (an important part of controlling watercolor painting). Some watercolor artists use sponges, but I prefer to use a washcloth that I can hold in one hand, ready for blotting. I buy them in bulk !

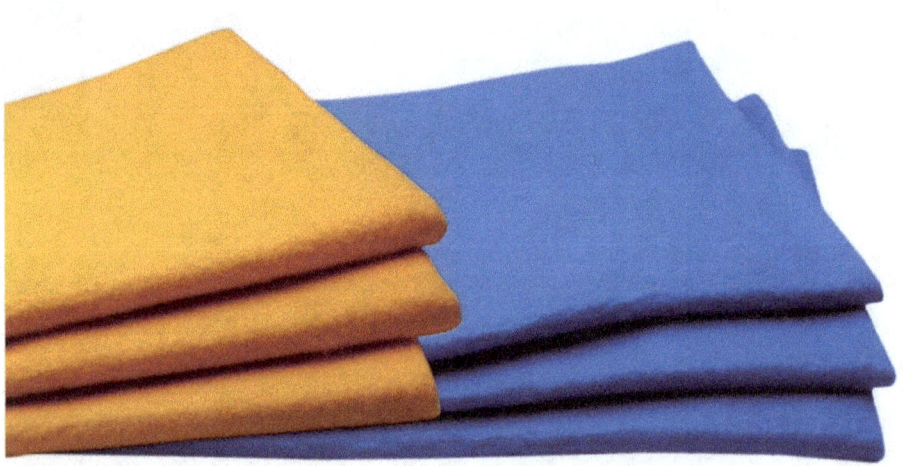

Watercolor Terms and Vocabulary (All the Jargon with Illustrations!)

Paint
- Binder – that which holds the paint together, such as linseed oil for oil painting, polymers for acrylics, gum arabic for watercolors and gouache.
- Classic or True – watercolors characterized by a luminous transparency: no matter how many layers of color are applied, the paint allows the light to penetrate and be reflected from the paper beneath.
- Filler or Inert Pigment – a powdered paint additive that does not change the shade or hue, but extends or otherwise imparts a special working quality to the paint. Fillers are used in lower and student grade paints as extenders, making the paint cheaper to produce, but of lower quality.
- Fugitive Colors – colors that can fade entirely, change color, darken to black, or other results when exposed to light over time. Some colors are still manufactured deliberately even with these unfortunate properties, as they are "historical" – the colors used by the old masters. Some artists want to use the same colors as Michaelangelo did.
- Lightfast Rating – a pigment's resistance to fading on long exposure to sunlight. Watercolors are rated lightfast on a scale of I-IV. I and II ratings are the most permanent. Inexpensive paints and student-grade paint lines often sacrifice lightfastness for cost.
- Gouache – opaque watercolor paints. (see Opacity). Some brands resemble gouache much more than watercolor.
- Gum Arabic – produced from the sap of the African acacia tree, available in crystalline form or an already prepared solution. It binds watercolor pigments when used with water and glycerine or honey.

Watercolor Terms and Vocabulary (All the Jargon with Illustrations!)

Paint
- Medium (pl. media or mediums) – 1) Most commonly, an artist's method of expression, such as ceramics, painting or glass. 2) a liquid added to a paint to thin, aid or slow drying, or alter the working qualities of the paint, without affecting its essential properties.
- Mixability – the ability for two paints to be combined to create a third. True pigments have better mixability than do hues.
- Non-staining colors – pigments that can be lifted cleanly (wet or re-wet) with little or no discoloration of the underlying paper fibers.
- Opacity, Opaque – impenetrable by light; not transparent or translucent. Denotes how much or little of the painting surface will show thru a layer of paint. True pigments tend to be more opaque, where hues tend to be more translucent.
- Organic – natural, or referring to nature in shape or form. Organic is the opposite of synthetic.
- Pan, Full Pan, or Half Pan – A semi-moist solid watercolor sold in a metal or plastic pan. Lighter weight and more portable than tube colors. Tube colors can be squeezed into pans.
- Pigment – Any coloring agent, made from natural or synthetic substances, used with a binder in paints or drawing materials. Pigments are derived from both natural and artificial sources. The earliest pigments were mined from colored clays of earth (ochres and umbers), but minerals and plants were also early sources for pigments. pigment: dry coloring matter, usually an insoluble powder, that's mixed with water and gum Arabic to create paint

Watercolor Terms and Vocabulary (All the Jargon with Illustrations!)

Paint
- Staining Colors – cannot be fully removed from paper. Staining colors permeate the fiber of the paper and leave a permanent tint. Some brands list the stain rating (I-IV), or check your hands after painting – the hardest colors to wash off are usually the staining colors.
- Synthetic – man-made materials. In paints, many synthetic pigments come from industries like automobiles. Synthetic brushes are made to resemble properties of natural bristles.
- Transparent vs translucent – both are penetrable by light; think of the difference between tempered glass and frosted glass – the diffusion of light through frosted glass is translucence.
- Tube color – liquid watercolor or gouache sold in a tube.
- Watercolor – paint that uses water-soluble gum arabic as the binder and water as the vehicle. Characterized by transparency. Also, the resulting painting.

Watercolor Terms and Vocabulary (All the Jargon with Illustrations!)

Color
- Analogous colors – related colors next to each other on the color wheel. Example: Yellow, Yellow Green, and Green.
- Complementary colors – hues directly opposite one another on a color wheel (for example, red and green, yellow and purple) which, when mixed together in proper proportions, produce a brown or neutral gray depending on proportions. These color combinations create the strongest possible contrast of color, and when placed close together, intensify the appearance of the other.
- Chroma – The purity or degree of saturation of a color; relative absence of white or gray in a color.
- Hue – The pure state of any color or a pure pigment that has not had white or black added to it. Hue: The color of a pigment or object. Not relating to tone or value.
- Intensity – a color's saturation, brightness or strength
- Muted – suppressing the full color value of a particular color.
- Primary colors – three colors (red, yellow, and blue) that are the basis for all other color combinations. Theoretically, pigment primaries can be mixed together to form all the other hues in the spectrum.
- Secondary colors – One of three colors created by mixing equal parts of two primary colors (red, blue, and yellow); the secondary colors are violet, orange, and green.

Watercolor Terms and Vocabulary (All the Jargon with Illustrations!)

Color
- Temperature – the warmness or coolness of a color, depending on where the color is situated on the color wheel
- Tertiary colors – those between a primary and secondary on the color wheel
- Tint – created by adding water or white to the original color; the more water added, the weaker the intensity
- Tone – a hue with gray added.
- Value – The lightness or darkness of tones or colors. White is the lightest value; black is the darkest. The value halfway between these extremes is middle gray.

Water Control !!!

1. Brush controls water
The water control of the paintbrush is mainly to use the paintbrush to dip in clean water and then dissolve the pigment for coloring. The watercolor pen has less bristle, toughness and good absorption. Usually after the pigment is melted, use the tip of the watercolor pen to dip in water Blends the smudge color.

2. Water control on paper
Water control on the paper surface means that before coloring, use a watercolor pen to absorb water, then wet the surface of the watercolor paper, let the watercolor paper absorb water, then dip the paint and brush it on the paper, the degree of smearing and diffusion of the paint is greater , creating a stronger sense of haze.

3. Color control and water control
Color control and water control refers to the method of diluting the pigment with water in the palette after dipping it into the palette, so as to change the depth of the color. For example, if we draw a piece of grass, some will smudge the distance first, and it can also be diluted with water The method of using light colors to paint the distance and dark colors to paint the near can create a sense of spatial hierarchy.

Water control is extremely important in watercolor painting. Whether we can control water well is also a key skill for us to paint watercolor paintings. The amount of water can determine the depth of color, and the way we control water can also determine the effect of the work.

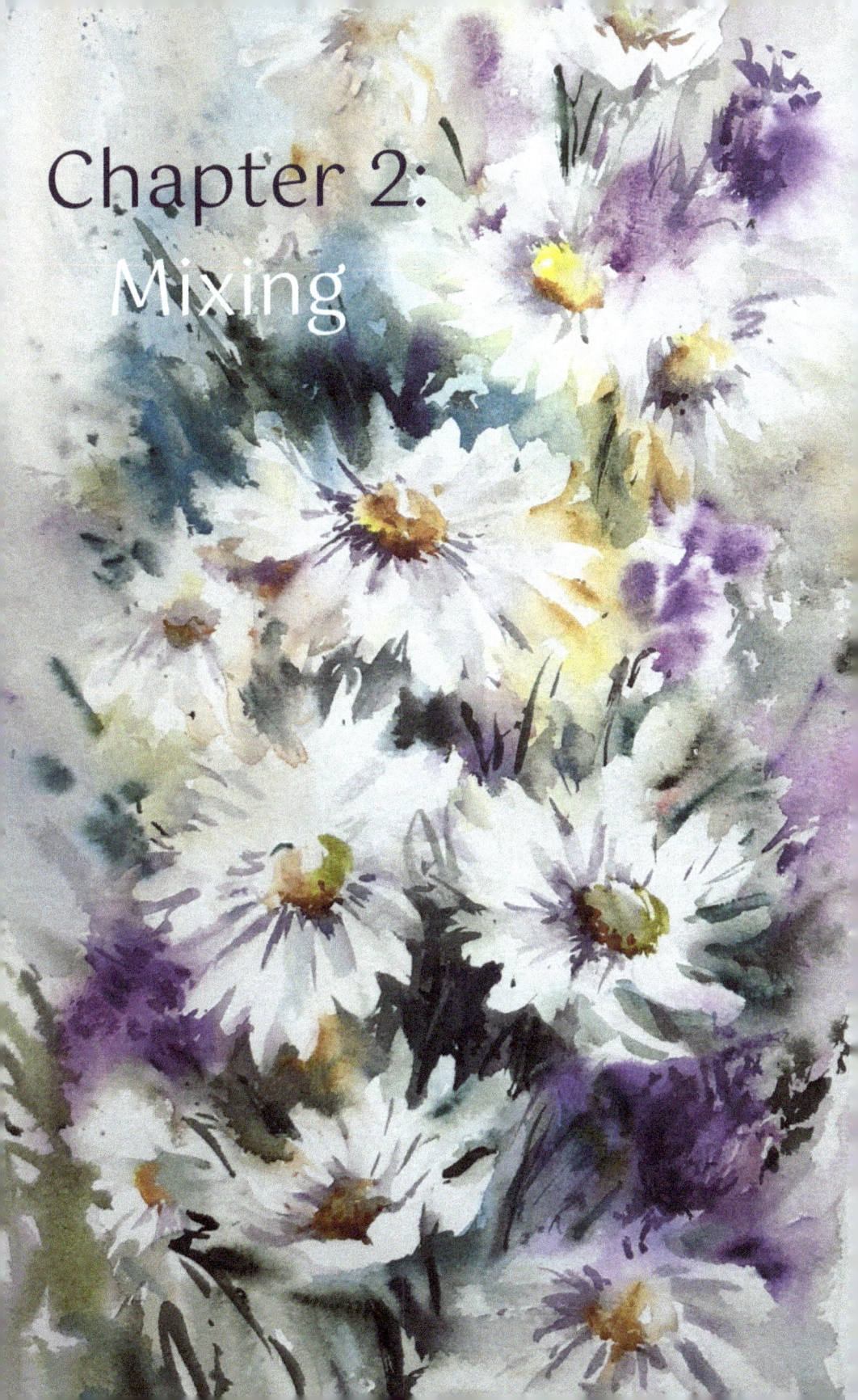

Chapter 2:
Mixing

The Essential Guide to Watercolor Mixing

Color theory: Primary, Secondary and Tertiary colors

- Don't' be put off – it's not as bad as it sounds ! The better you know some basic color theory, the more easily and quickly you'll be able to mix colors from your palette.

- The basics of color theory can be clearly understood by means of a color wheel:

- The color wheel is an incredibly useful tool for watercolor artists. It shows us what color can be produced by mixing adjacent colors with each other. Traditional color wheels are made up of three categories of colors: primary, secondary and tertiary.

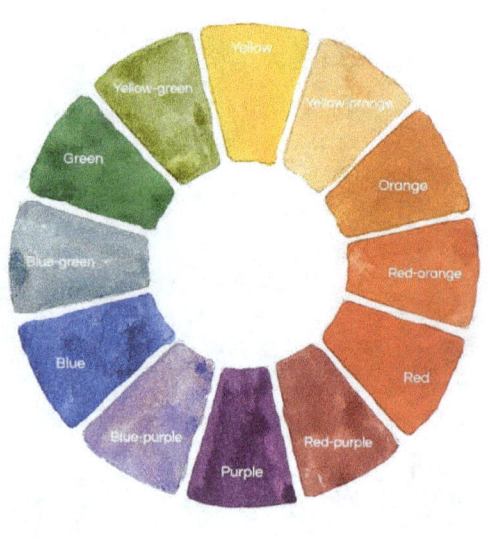

- It all begins with primary colors. The primary colors are the starting point for any color wheel.

- **yellow**
- **red**
- **blue**

The Essential Guide to Watercolor Mixing

Color theory: Primary, Secondary and Tertiary colors

- Primary colors are the foundation of color mixing because these three color pigments cannot be mixed by the combination of any other colors.

- Next we have secondary colors. Most of us are already familiar with these simple mixing formulas:

- **yellow + red = orange**
- **red + blue = purple**
- **blue + yellow = green**

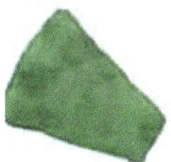
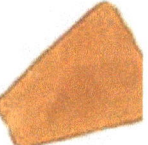
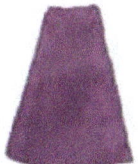

The Essential Guide to Watercolor Mixing

Color theory: Primary, Secondary and Tertiary colors

- The final category is tertiary colors. These are achieved by mixing the primary and secondary colors which are adjacent to each other on the color wheel:

- **yellow + orange = yellow-orange**
- **red + orange = red-orange**
- **red + purple = red-purple**
- **blue + purple = blue-purple**
- **blue + green = blue-green**
- **yellow + green= yellow-green**

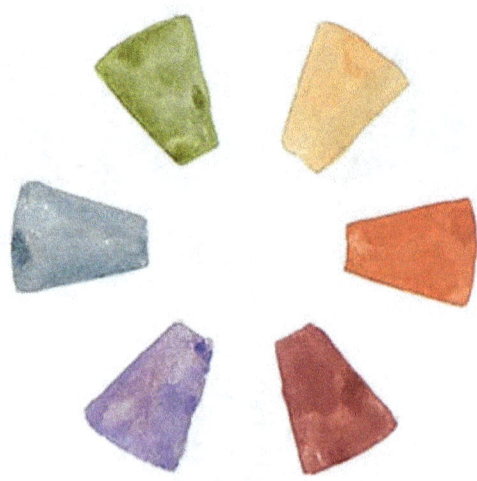

(note: traditionally the naming convention for tertiary colors always begins with the primary color, then the secondary: red-orange, yellow-green, etc.)

The Essential Guide to Watercolor Mixing

What are warm and cool colors ?

- Warm colors are those that are situated on one side of the color wheel and include yellow, orange, and red.

- Cool colors are on the opposite side of the color wheel and include purple, blue, and green.

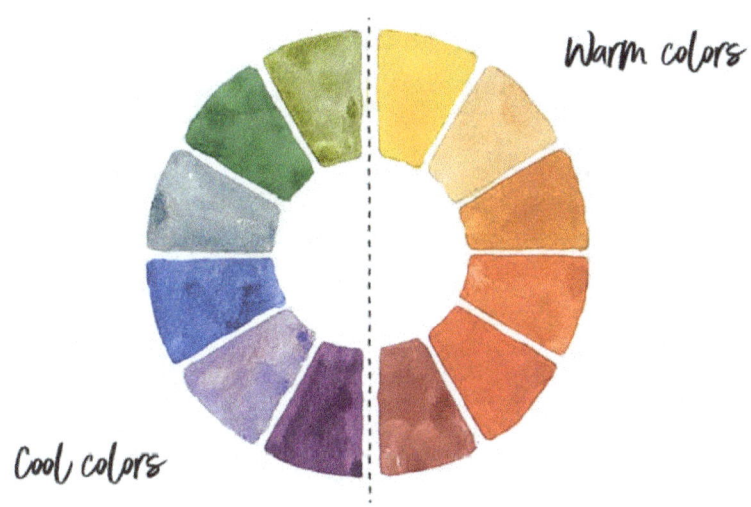

This is where a lot of people get confused. How do you identify whether a color is warm or cool ?

The Essential Guide to Watercolor Mixing

What are warm and cool colors ?

- Color wheels can help us with this. The color wheel below is based on two sets of primary colors. There's a warm and a cool version of each primary color. So we have a warm and a cool yellow, a warm and a cool red, etc. I've also painted the secondary color mixes in between each set of primary colors.

- The position of a color on the color wheel represents whether it is warm or cool:

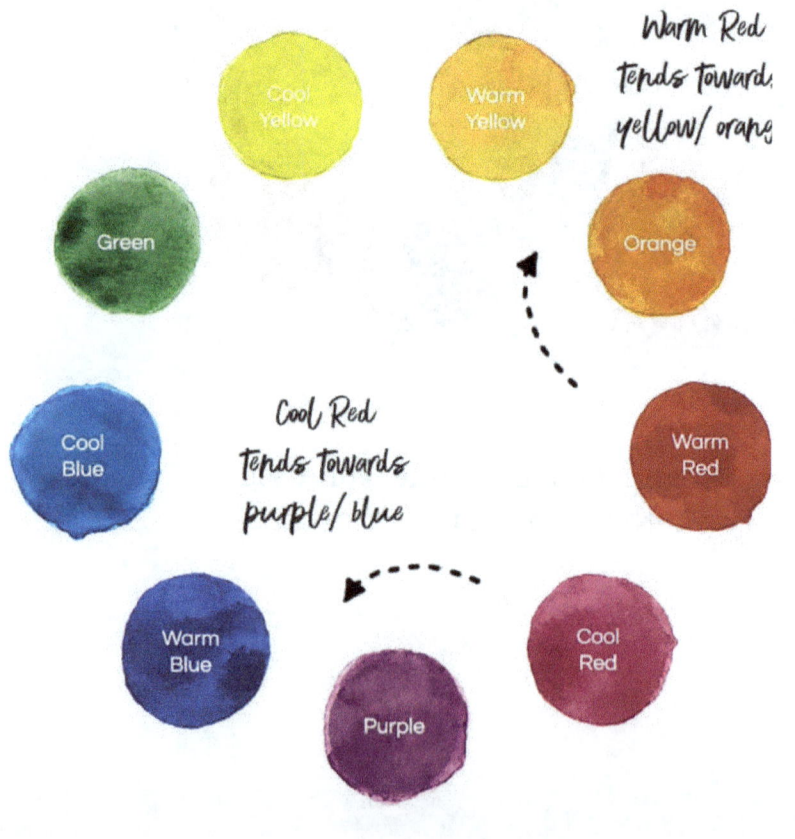

The Essential Guide to Watercolor Mixing

Mixing pure saturated secondary colors

- Even though color theory tells us that red+blue = purple, not every red mixed with every blue makes a pure purple.
- As mentioned above, your paints can have a warm or cool bias. Let's say you want to mix a pure green color. The simple mixing recipe yellow + blue can sometimes produce surprising results, depending on the color bias of the paints you choose:
- So, do you know how to mix a saturated secondary color such as a pure saturated green or saturated purple ?
- Take another look at the color wheel we used earlier:

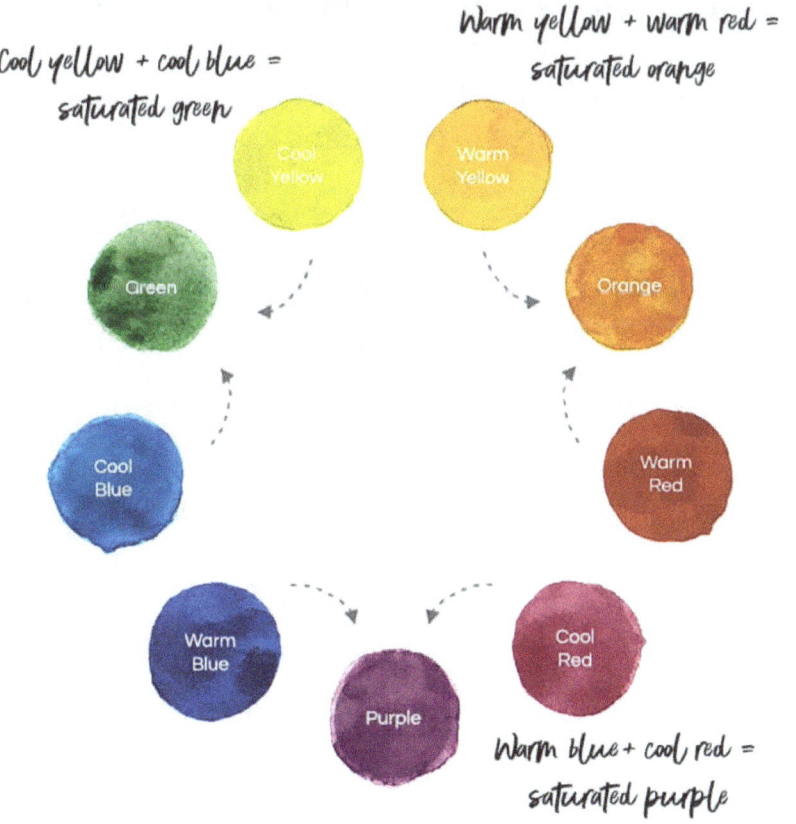

The Essential Guide to Watercolor Mixing

Mixing pure saturated secondary colors

- As you can see above, the secondary colors, orange, purple, and green are bright and saturated.
- To mix them you need to use a specific combination of two primary colors:
- To mix a very saturated orange you use the primary colors which are **closest to orange: warm yellow + warm red**
- To mix a very saturated purple you use those primary colors which are **closest to purple: cool red + warm blue**
- To mix a very saturated green you use primary colors which are **closest to green: cool blue + cool yellow**
- You may be wondering what happens if you break this formula and mix different primary colors together. For example if you mix a cool blue and a warm yellow you get the following mixture:

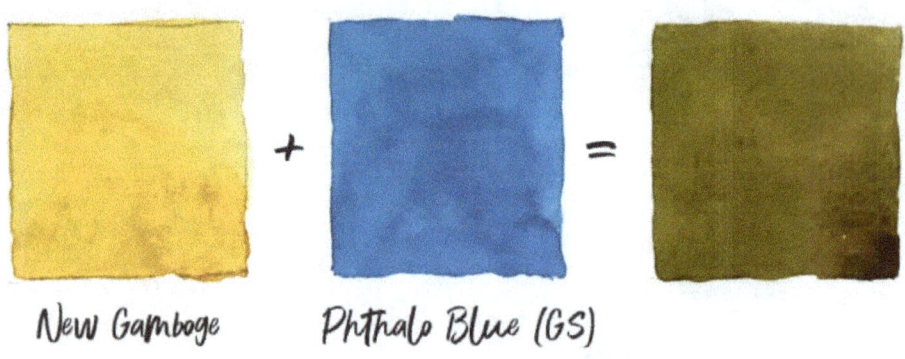

New Gamboge Phthalo Blue (GS)

The Essential Guide to Watercolor Mixing

Mixing neutralized hues using compound colors

- You can obtain neutral colors by mixing combinations of warm and cool primary colors which are located further away from the desired color on the color wheel. Mixing in this way produces compound colors. These are colors which include a trace of all three primary colors
- Let's take the example of purple.
- You can create a muted compound purple by using the primaries furthest from purple on the color wheel:
- For instance, mixing warm red + cool blue produces a desaturated neutralized purple:

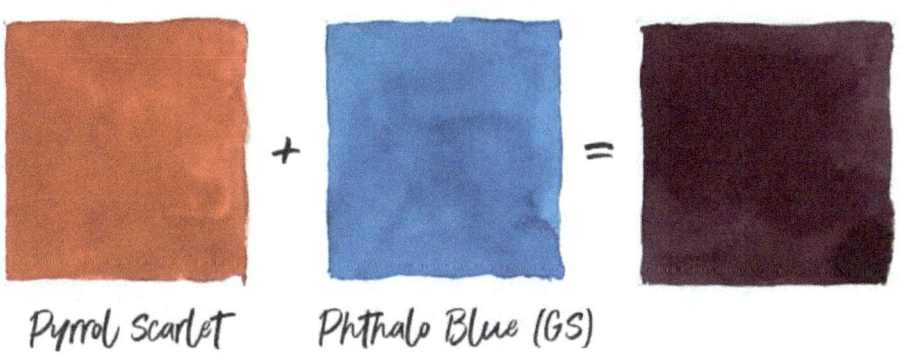

Pyrrol Scarlet   Phthalo Blue (GS)

The Essential Guide to Watercolor Mixing

Mixing neutralized hues using complementary colors

- Using the same six primary colors you can push your color mixing further by implementing complementary color mixing. This method allows you to neutralize and desaturate your colors to produce a vast range of grays and earth tones.
- A complementary color is any color on the opposite side of the color wheel.
- The complement of yellow is purple.
- The complement of red is green.
- When you mix any color with its complementary color you get a neutralized gray or earth hue.
- Here are a couple of examples:
- As a quick rule of thumb, try to remember the following complementary combinations:

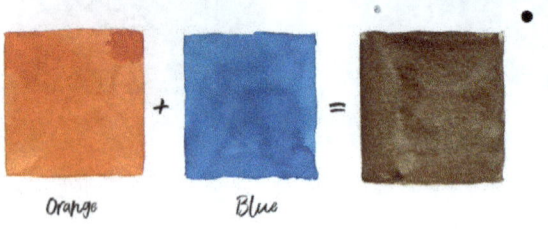

- As a quick rule of thumb, try to remember the following complementary combinations:

- Yellow + Purple
- Red + Green
- Blue + Orange

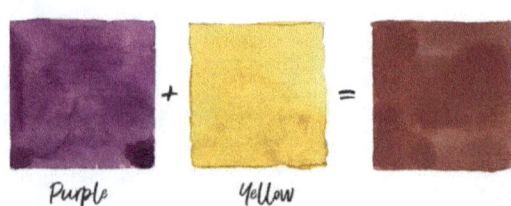

The Essential Guide to Watercolor Mixing

Using a limited color palette

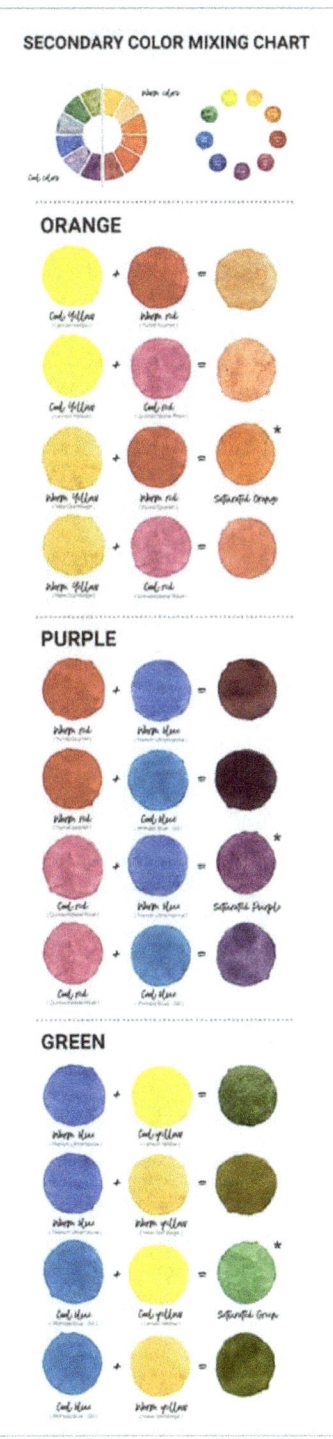

- As you probably now realize, the primary colors yellow, red, and blue, are the backbone of any watercolor palette. Primary paint colors are an indispensable part of your palette because you cannot mix primaries from any other paint colors. Almost every possible color mixture can be obtained using just a few primary color paints.

- The chart below illustrates this mixing range:

The Essential Guide to Watercolor Mixing

Using the color wheel as a guide to mixing

- Let's say you want to reproduce a color similar to Raw Sienna.
- First locate the approximate hue you want to mix on the circumference of the color wheel. Raw Sienna is a warm color somewhere between red and yellow. This hue is probably more yellow than red, so your starting point on the color wheel would be yellow-orange.
- Having made these judgements I can now locate my target color on the color wheel.

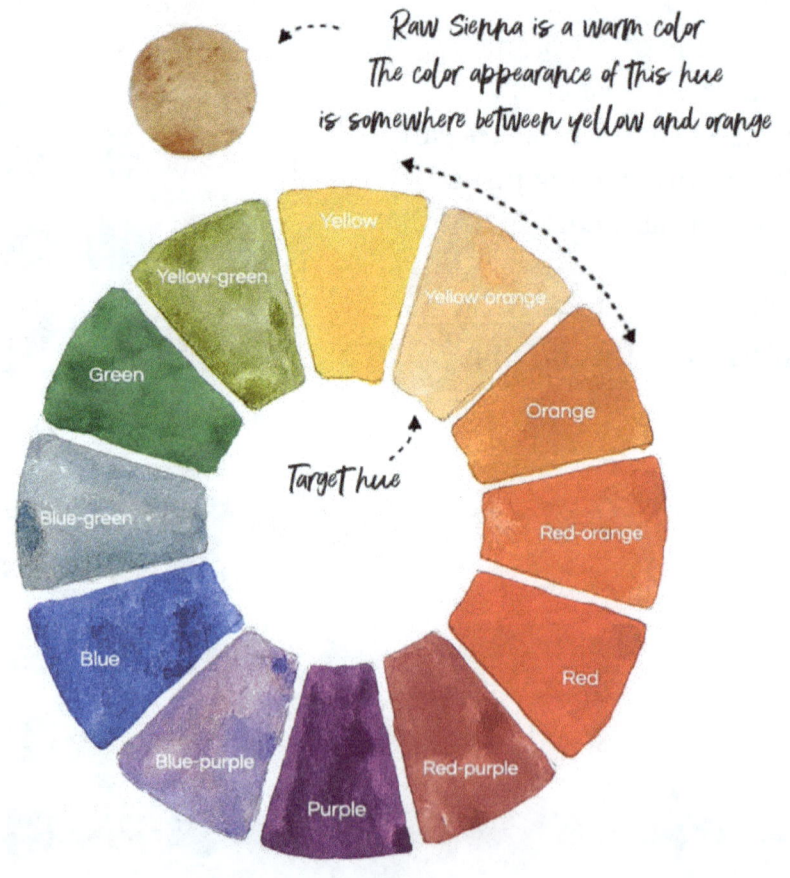

The Essential Guide to Watercolor Mixing

Tonal Adjustments

- Tone is the relative lightness or darkness of a color.
- With watercolors, the brightest most saturated colors are the pure pigments that come straight from the tubes. You cannot make these colors any brighter.
- This kind of saturated color is said to have a strong tonal value.
- If you want to "tone down" your colors to make them lighter, it's simply a matter of adding more water to dilute the mixture and thereby lighten the tones.
- Because watercolor paint is a transparent medium the lightness of a color comes from the underlying white paper.
- It's possible that you have a tube of white or black paint in your watercolor collection. You may be tempted to use one of these to darken or lighten your colors. But black or white paint will deaden your colors.
- In watercolor painting you control the level of tone by changing the ratio of paint to water.
- Correct tone is one of the essential components to successful painting. If the relative tones in your scene are true, you can produce a believable sense of space, light and form.

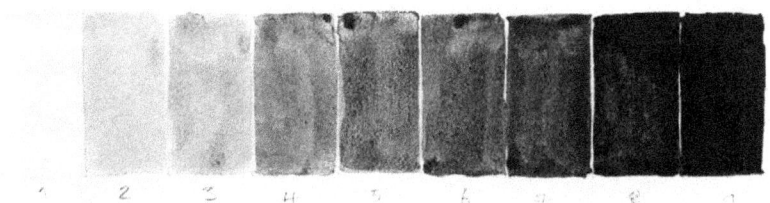

Chapter 3: Techniques

Unmissable Watercolor Techniques (EVERYTHING You Need!)

What are the Different Watercolor Techniques?

1. **Wet on wet**
2. **Wet-on-Dry**
3. **Dry on Wet**
4. **Dry on Dry**
5. **Charging-in (Feathering)**

This is essentially a wet-on-wet technique. The wetness of both paper and paintbrush changes the resulting effects.

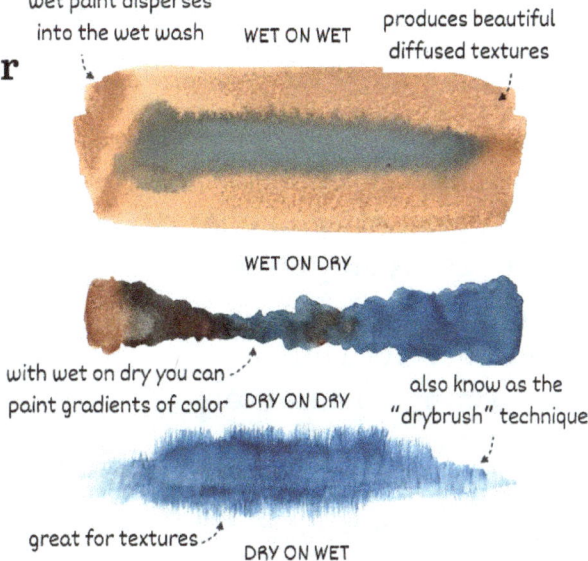

WET ON WET — wet paint disperses into the wet wash — produces beautiful diffused textures

WET ON DRY — with wet on dry you can paint gradients of color

DRY ON DRY — also know as the "drybrush" technique — great for textures

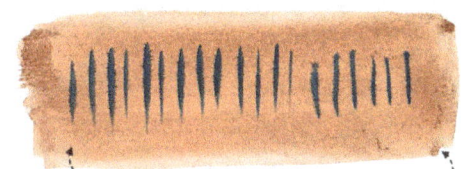

DRY ON WET — produces subtle details — paint with a slightly damp brush on a wet surface

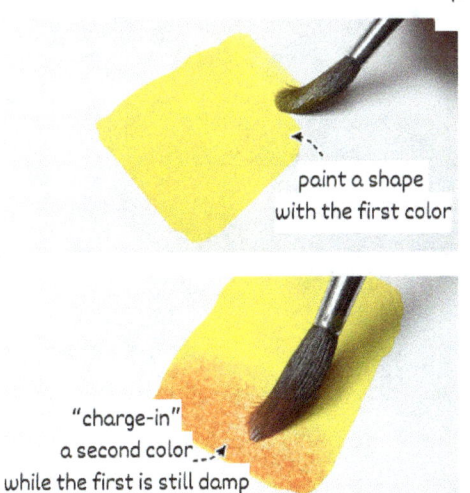

paint a shape with the first color

"charge-in" a second color while the first is still damp

Unmissable Watercolor Techniques (EVERYTHING You Need!)

What are the Different Watercolor Techniques?

- **Glazing**

Glazing sounds like a complicated technique, but it's actually quite simple. Glazing is another word for "layering." The notion of layering in watercolors is essential, as you'll probably discover the more you paint. Unlike a lot of other art mediums, watercolors are transparent. This means that each brushstroke you lay down on paper is visible underneath every subsequent layer of paint. This transparency is what gives rise to the technique of glazing.

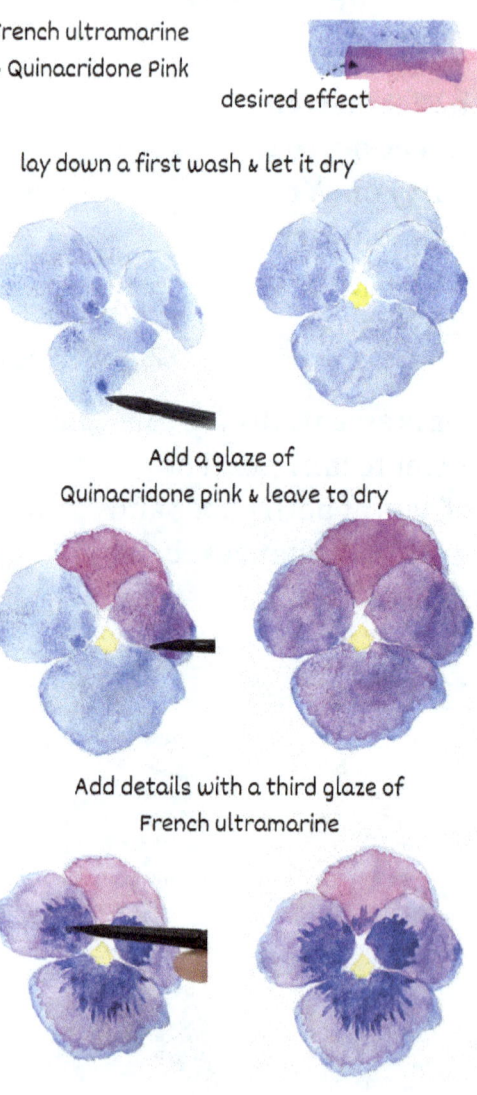

Unmissable Watercolor Techniques (EVERYTHING You Need!)

What are the Different Watercolor Techniques?

- **Watercolor Salt Effects**

Using salt on watercolor is a method of adding texture to a painting. Salt has absorbent qualities. To use this technique, salt is sprinkled onto a wet wash of color, and the salt absorbs the paint in the surrounding area.

In this way, adding salt to a damp wash of watercolor creates bursts of feathery textures around the grains of salt.

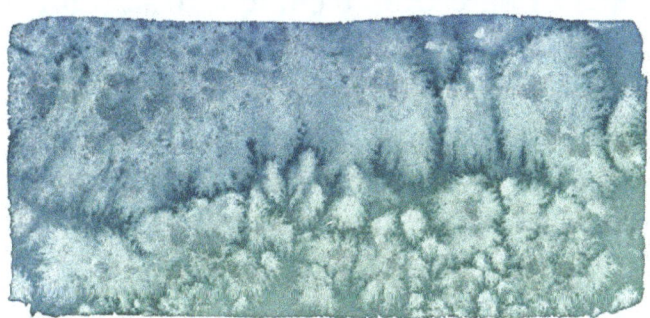

- **Watercolor Spray Bottle Technique**

I always have a spray bottle with clear water nearby when painting. It's a quick and easy method for adding speckled texture to watercolor paintings. You can produce a splatter texture by vaporizing droplets of water into a damp area of watercolor.

When the water drops hit the wet surface, the water spreads outward. It pushes the pigment away, leaving behind a lighter-toned speckle on the surface. (This is the same phenomenon as "watercolor blooms").

Unmissable Watercolor Techniques (EVERYTHING You Need!)

What are the Different Watercolor Techniques?

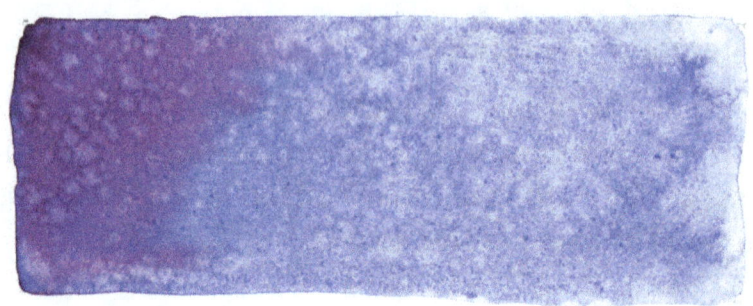

- **Watercolor Dripping**

Dripping is a fun watercolor technique to add abstract flowing drips of color to a painting. A very wet application of paint can be encouraged to trickle down the page using the help of gravity.

This is more of an illustrative style of texture creation in watercolors. It yields a very interesting graphic look to a painting!

Watercolors' watery, fluid nature makes this method unique compared to other mediums.

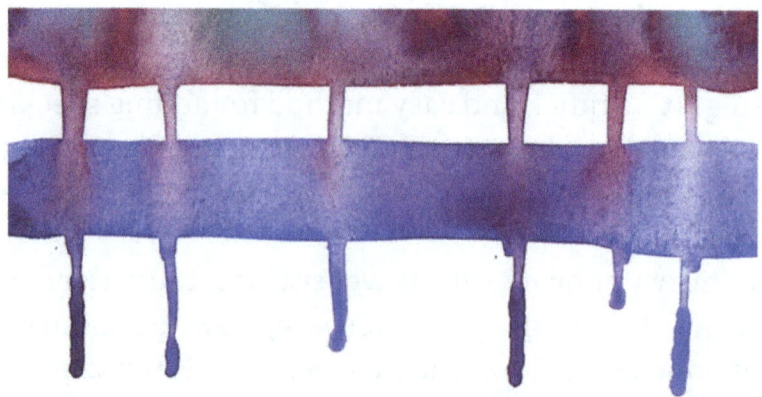

Unmissable Watercolor Techniques (EVERYTHING You Need!)

What are the Different Watercolor Techniques?

- **Watercolor Bloom Texture Method**

Watercolor blooms (also known as cauliflowers or blossoms) are often viewed as a mistake. They occur when paint or water flows back into a drying wash, causing a feathery-looking texture.

But when you know how to control the appearance of blooms, this phenomenon can be deliberately used to add interesting texture to a painting.

The effect remains somewhat random and uncontrolled, but this haphazard quality is one of the beautiful aspects of watercolor!

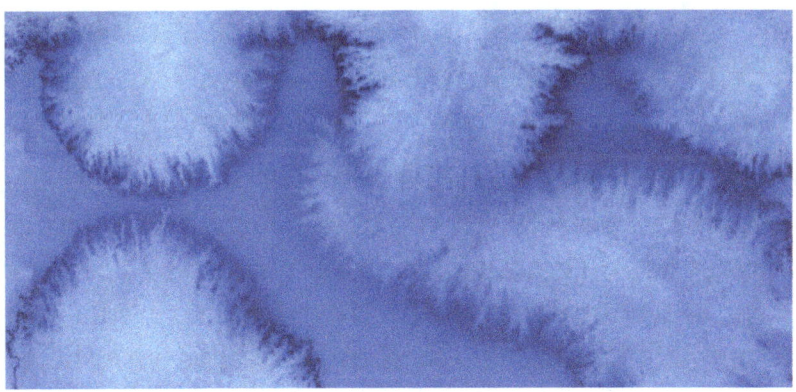

Unmissable Watercolor Techniques (EVERYTHING You Need!)

Blending Methods

- **Watercolor Blending Methods**

Blending (going from dark to light) is one of the most challenging techniques in watercolor. It requires a certain amount of brush control and a well-practiced technique. But blending is essential for gradually transitioning from one tone or color to another and giving your artwork a sense of three-dimensional form.

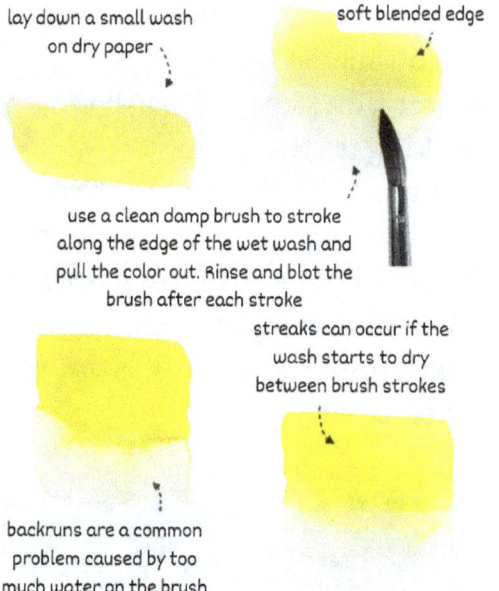

- Rinse your brush, then blot it on a paper towel to remove most of the moisture (If you use a brush loaded with clear water, you will get a backrun that produces a feathery pattern in your damp wash). Next, brush the edge you want to blend and pull the paint outwards with the moist brush. The pigment will disperse into the dampness and will be diluted in strength. Continue to clean and blot your brush repeatedly and brush the edge until it blends completely.

- All of this needs to be done relatively quickly before the paint has time to dry.

Unmissable Watercolor Techniques (EVERYTHING You Need!)

Washes

- **The Flat Wash**

To perform a successful flat wash, there are two different methods that most watercolor artists use. Perhaps the most frequent is to use a wet on dry approach. But it's also possible to make a great flat wash using a wet on wet technique.

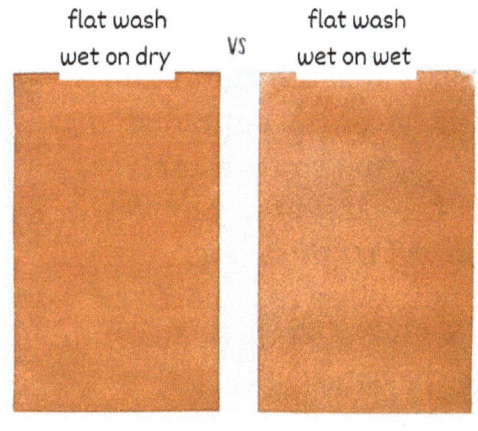

- **The Graded Wash**

Graded washes can be painted wet on dry or wet on wet. The method is practically the same as for a flat wash, but instead of applying the same strength of paint over the entire wash area, we gradually add clear water to the paint mix so that it becomes more and more diluted.

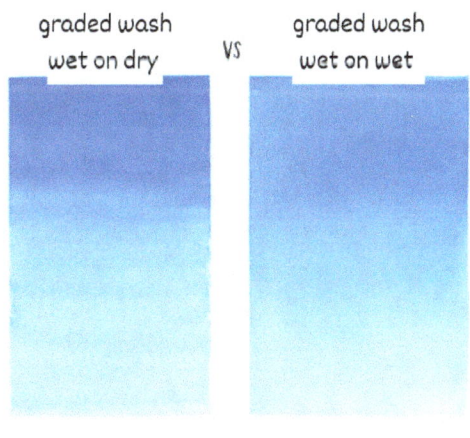

Unmissable Watercolor Techniques (EVERYTHING You Need!)

Washes

- **The Variegated Wash**

The technique used is very much the same as for painting a flat or graded wash, and you can apply either a wet on dry or wet on wet method. The colors bleed together in a slightly unpredictable way producing very appealing results.

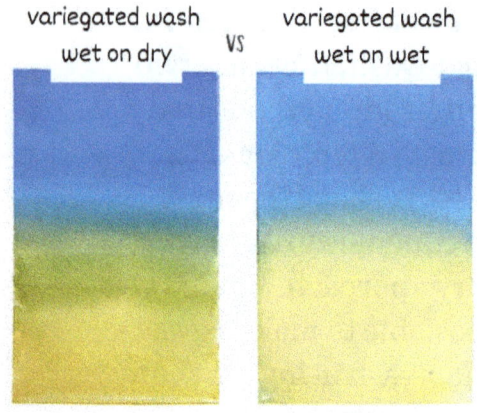

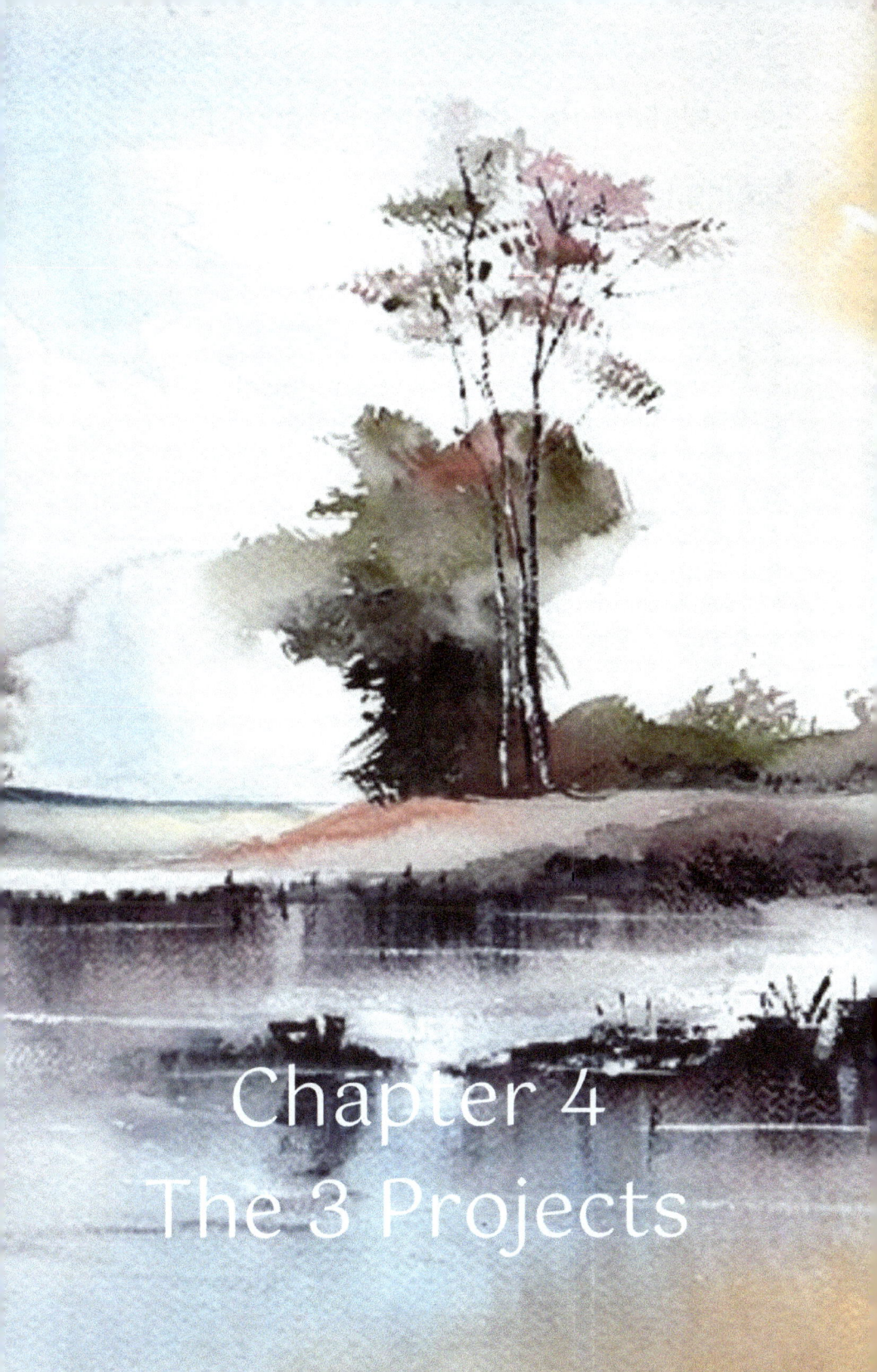

Chapter 4
The 3 Projects

Easy Watercolor Painting Tutorial for Beginners

Supplies:

- 8" by 5.5" watercolor paper
- Watercolor brushes: size 14 and one liner brush
- Watercolors (ultramarine blue, Indigo, sap green, may green, naple yellow, yellow ocher, payne's gray)
- White paint
- 2 jars of water
- Rough cloth/tissue
- Palette to mix all your colors
- Pencil, eraser and masking tape

Easy Watercolor Painting Tutorial for Beginners

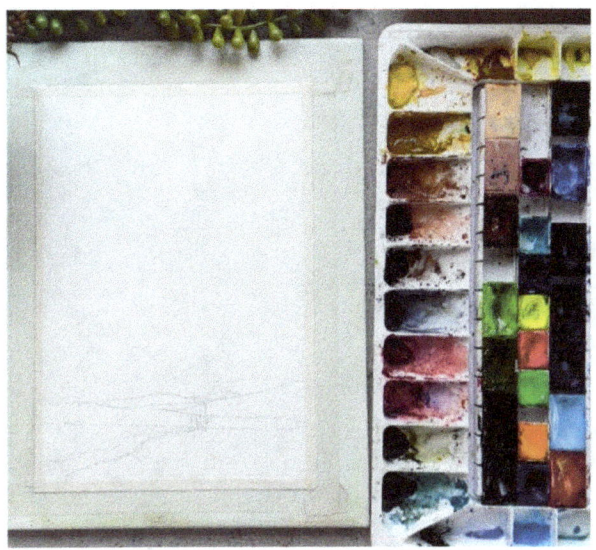

Step 1: Sketch Your Landscape Composition

- As we majorly want to focus on the sky, we will leave ⅔ of the paper for the sky and the rest of the bottom area will be for the land.
- Apply masking tape on all sides of your paper and thoroughly press it down so that there is no gap between the paper and the masking tape.
- Once masking tape is applied, start lightly sketching small mountains from the bottom of your page. Between those mountains, draw a small river stream.

Easy Watercolor Painting Tutorial for Beginners

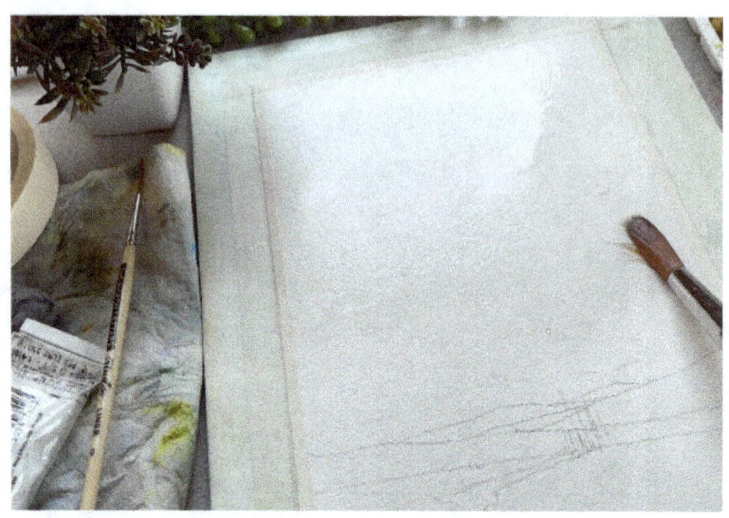

Step 2: Prepare Colors and Wet the Paper

- As we will be painting the sky using a wet-on-wet watercolor technique, it is advisable to first prepare the colors for the sky so that you don't waste time while painting. So for the shadows in the clouds, mix 50% of Paynes gray with 50% either white gouache or white watercolor. For the sky, mix 80% of ultramarine with 20% white. Adding white will help the color to spread a little less on the paper, thus making it easy for you to control paint and water on paper while using the wet-on-wet technique.
- Once our colors are ready, start wetting the sky area. . You see the shine on the paper? That's how wet your paper should be.

Easy Watercolor Painting Tutorial for Beginners

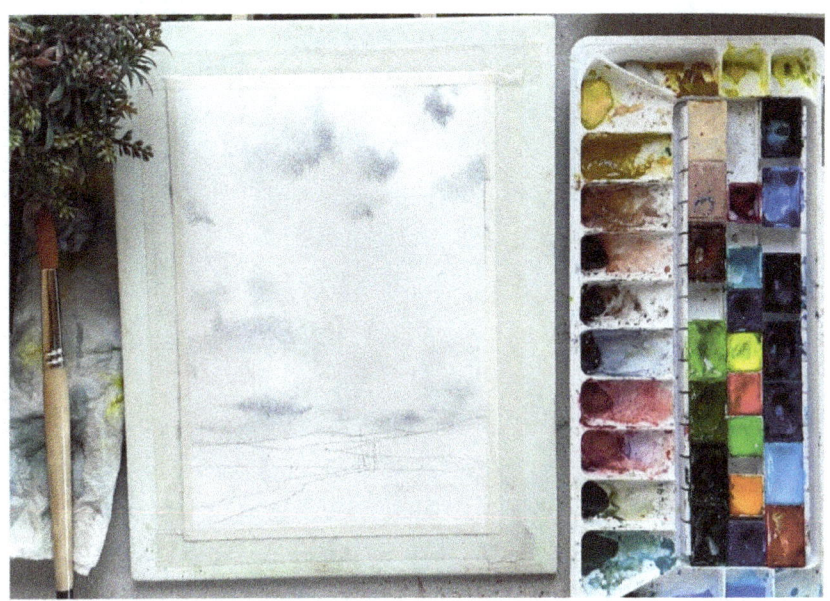

Step 3: Paint the Cloud's Shadow

- Before you start applying the colors, tilt your paper at a 30 degree angle by just placing masking tape or any object below. This will help the colors and water to flow downward. If you see excess water flowing down, just grab a tissue and lift off the extra water. Then start applying the gray color that we mixed earlier on the wet paper, leaving the gaps in between.

Easy Watercolor Painting Tutorial for Beginners

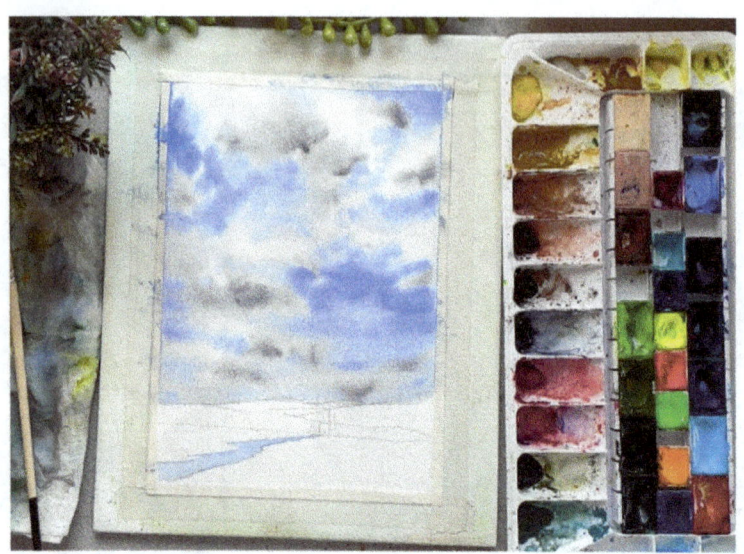

Step 4: Paint the Sky and Water Stream

- Once we have painted the shadow of the clouds, we will start painting the sky. Grab the blue color which we mixed earlier and start applying that color on the wet paper, leaving white gaps near the shadows you painted. Once you start applying the blue color, you will see clouds and sky come to life and everything will make sense now. Later, use the same color but dilute it a little by adding water and paint the water stream.

Tips
- Use a thick consistency of blue paint so it spreads a little less.
- You can always use clean tissue to lift off the blue paint in case you feel there is not enough white on the sky
- - or - you can always use a damp brush to lift off the paint too

Easy Watercolor Painting Tutorial for Beginners

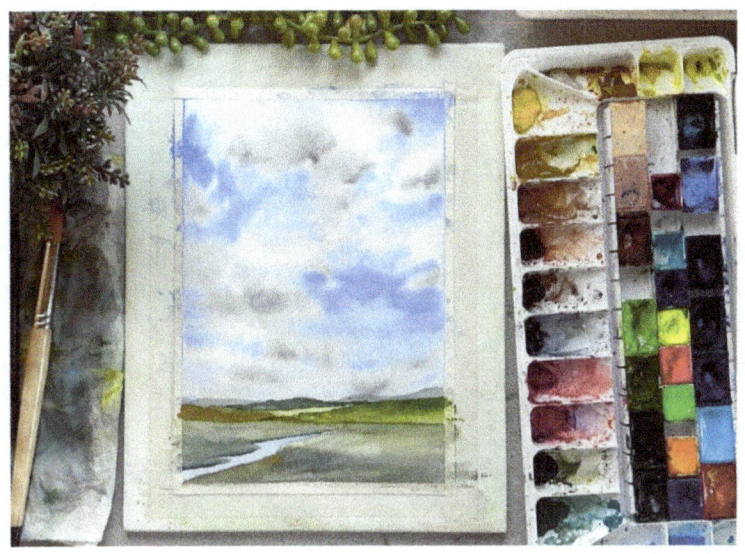

Step 5: Paint the Background Mountains

- Start painting all the layers of the mountains as well as the foreground with different shades of green. Use water and a little bit of yellow ochre to make greens lighter, and the same way, use indigo to make it a little darker. Let each layer dry before you paint the adjacent mountain. Otherwise, the colors will flow into each other. Use dark dull colors to paint the mountains which are at the very end and as you come forward, use bright greens, as that's where sunlight is hitting the ground.

Easy Watercolor Painting Tutorial for Beginners

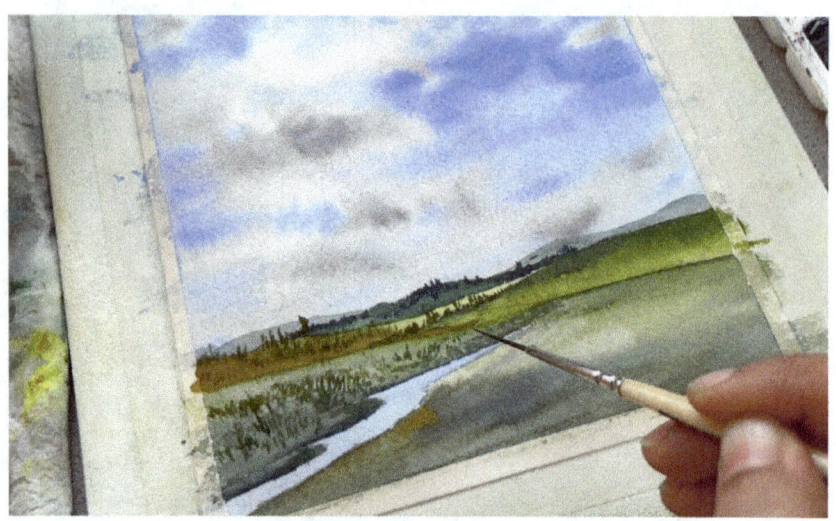

Step 6: Add Foreground Details

- Now take a liner brush or small size 1 brush and start adding tiny little grasses, bushes and trees. Use different shades of greens to do that. This will sure take a little bit of time and patience but the end result will be phenomenal so don't hurry this step.

Easy Watercolor Painting Tutorial for Beginners

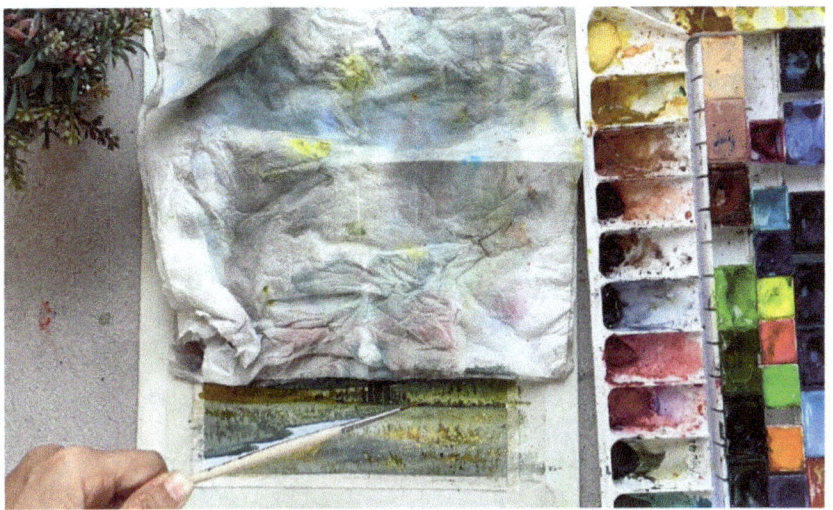

Step 7: Add Splatters for Interest

- Before you add splatters, cover the sky area with paper or tissue. Then we want the splatters to be small so we will use a smaller brush to do that. So first load your brush with paint and then either use your hands or other brush and start taping on the brush with paint. You will see drops on paint fall on the paper. So repeat this step with each color, i.e. sap green, yellow ochre and naples yellow.

Easy Watercolor Painting Tutorial for Beginners

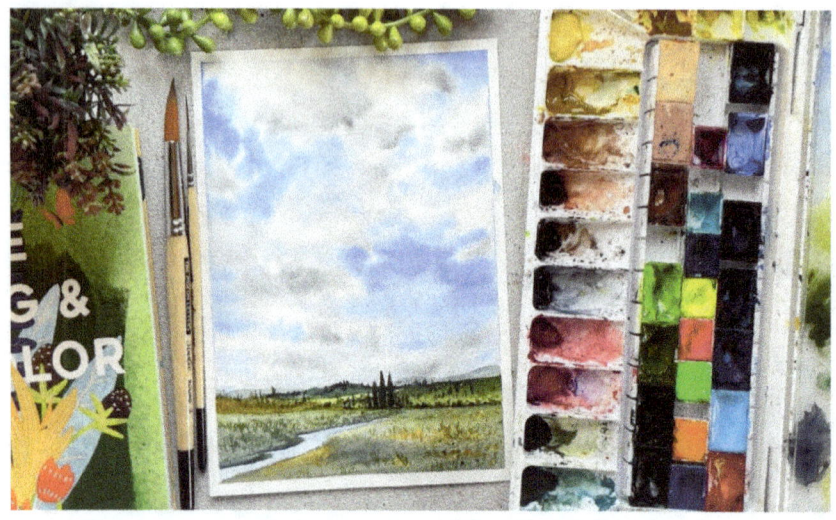

Step 8: Remove the Masking Tape

- And we are done! Now let everything dry completely. Once it has dried, remove the masking tape at an angle, which is away from the paper so that you don't end up tearing it. And ta-da we are done painting a beautiful summer day landscape painting using watercolors.
- Thank you so much for painting along with me. I hope you enjoyed learning. Now it's your turn to paint and have some fun. If you happen to share do tag me I would love to see your amazing work. Until next time!

A Step-By-Step Watercolor Landscape Tutorial

Step 1: Gather and prepare all supplies.

- For this painting, I painted in my sketchbook and I used blue painter's tape to mark off the borders.

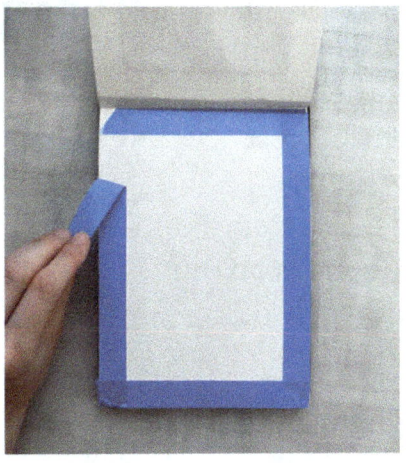

Step 2: Carefully observe your landscape.

- There's no shortcut for this one. You'll have to take a minute and observe your landscape. Maybe more than a minute. Close your eyes, and imagine what it would look like on your paper. Then, look at your paper.

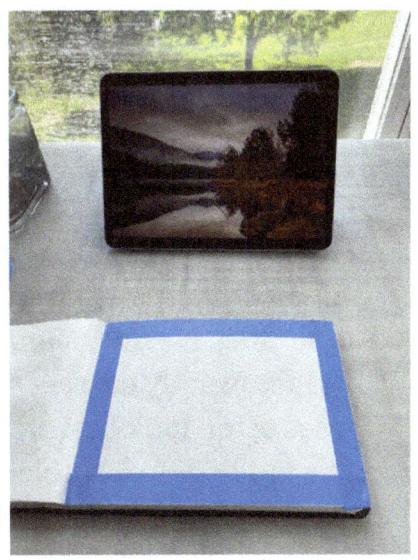

A Step-By-Step Watercolor Landscape Tutorial

Step 2: Carefully observe your landscape.

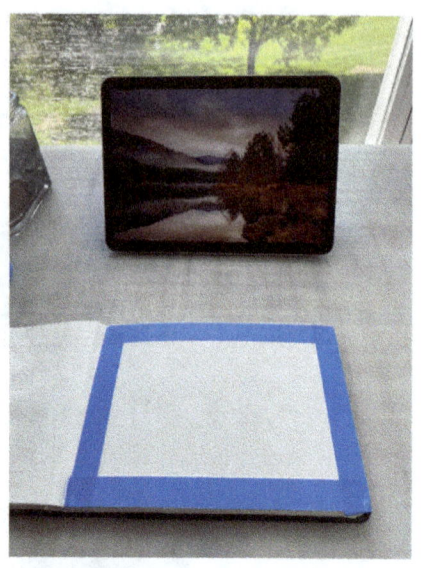

- When I start a landscape, I usually start with the horizon line, and sketch that lightly. I generally draw the land first, starting with the biggest shapes or areas. In this particular piece, I started sketching the big trees on the shore on the right side of the image.
- I observe the photo and see that the tree/shoreline area takes up about 1/3 of the width, draw a little line guessing where the shoreline ends, and sketch within that area. There are 3 "major" or large/obvious trees on the right, so I sketch those first. Then I work around the smaller trees.
- Next, I draw the mountains in the very back (there are 2, and they're very basic). Next is the treeline right in front of the mountains. Then I may go and sketch out details such as the rocks in front.
- Important note: I rarely draw any details in the sky. This is because it's not as important for me to get the cloud shapes exactly correct, and because I believe watercolor skies often look best without pencil lines visible at all. If you are uncomfortable with this idea, then definitely sketch your sky: but I recommend keeping it light!

A Step-By-Step Watercolor Landscape Tutorial

Step 3: Paint from "back" to "front."

- What I mean by this is: start with the objects that sit in the "back" of your image if you imagine it as a multi-layered diorama right in front of you. Your brain will instantly recognize the mountains as the furthest object away, then the treeline directly in front of the mountains, then the lake, etc. I decided to start with the sky on this one, so that I can visually "map" out where things will go underneath.

- Since this sky is dark at the top edge, it's easy to map out where things should go: the dark swirls form almost a "cone" that points down to the landscape, and you can fit the mountains and trees underneath. I also find this a good time to paint the reflection the lake. This can be challenging to get exactly right, but don't beat yourself up trying to make it an exact reflection.

- The primary colors I used for the sky were Payne's Gray and Yellow Ochre.

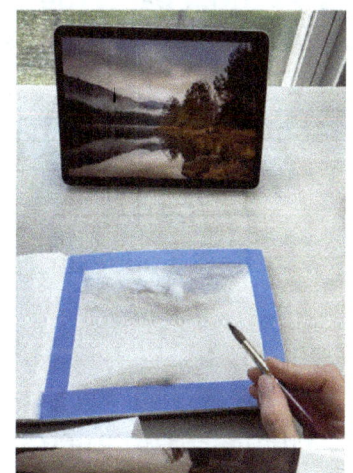

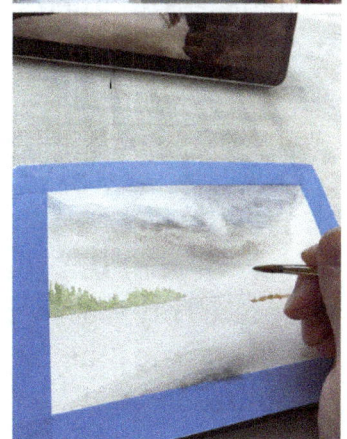

A Step-By-Step Watercolor Landscape Tutorial

Step 3: Paint from "back" to "front."

- Well, it looks like I broke my own rules, sorry about that! I painted the treeline next, and I see why: there is a layer of mist that is separating the trees from the mountains, and since I already painted the lake, I wanted to paint a "midpoint" between the mountains and lake so that I had a general idea of how big each one should be. I used Sap Green for the trees.
- Next up, I paint the reflection of the treeline in the water. I painted the trees to be more sharp/detailed about the lake, then used extra water on my brush to "blur" the trees' reflection and make it more watery in appearance.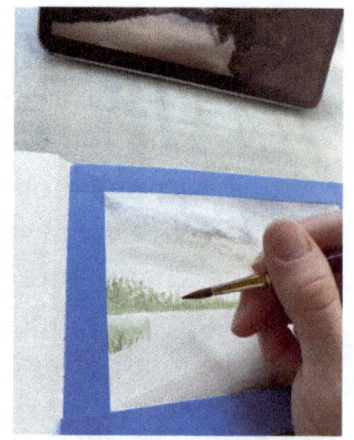
- Important thing to remember: objects in the back will inherently be lighter/bluer in color; and they will be less detailed. This is a natural phenomena to denote visualizing distance, and it's true in real life too. It will greatly add depth to your work to keep this in mind when you're painting the "back" of your image first. I used Payne's Gray with some touches of Ultramarine Blue for the mountains.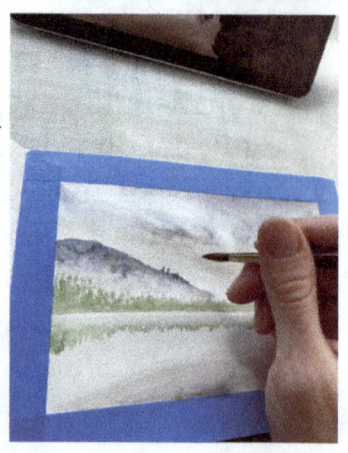

A Step-By-Step Watercolor Landscape Tutorial

Step 4: Paint the shoreline on the right, with darker and sharper detail.

- After you've painted the sky, mountains, and treeline (and their corresponding reflections), I would move on next to the shoreline on the right of the image. I mixed a burnt sienna with some yellow ochre to make the dirt color.

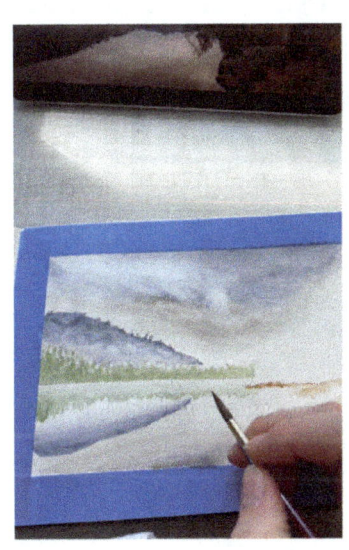

- As you can see here, I am skittish about filling large areas of color. One of my habits as a painter is that I paint just "within" the area I think I need to fill, just in case I need to come back later and add on to it. This is a cautious way of painting to prevent you from accidentally filling in too large of an area that may encroach on other objects in the painting, like a tree or something else. Yes, I've learned this the hard way!

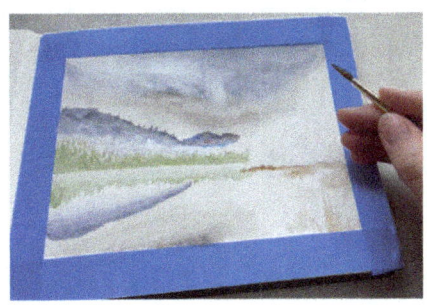

A Step-By-Step Watercolor Landscape Tutorial

Step 5: Paint the trees, from "trunk" then to "limb."

- Time for the trees to come in! Ok, When I say paint from "trunk" to "limb," what I mean is aim your brushstrokes from the center mass of the tree (where the trunk is/would be), to the outer branches. Flick your wrist so that the brushstrokes are horizontal, originating at the center of the tree, then the strokes get smaller the further away from the center of the tree you go.
- For this particular painting, I "dabbed" a dampish brush loaded with paint (Sap Green and Viridian) to make broken, uneven, organic branch shapes, as you can see above.

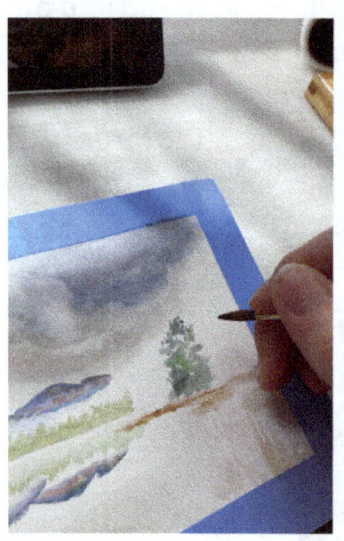
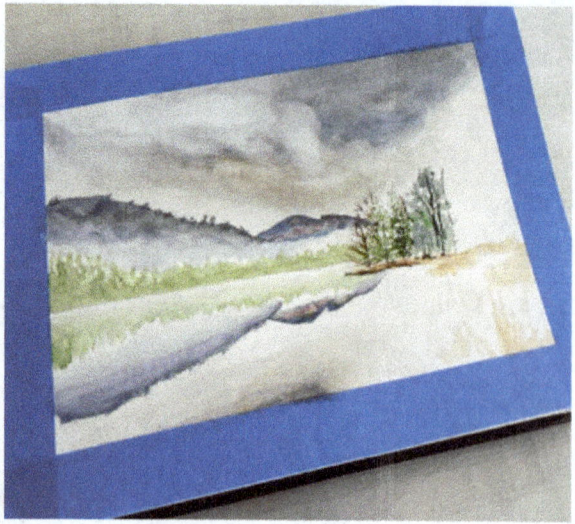

A Step-By-Step Watercolor Landscape Tutorial

Step 5: Paint the trees, from "trunk" then to "limb."

- Once I do initial layers of the lighter, abstracted branches, then I look at my reference photo carefully to see where there are trees with darker, more distinct branches. Once my paper is dry, that's when I use my small 000 brush and add the darker trunks and branches (with burnt umber, burnt sienna, sap green and some ultramarine blue).
- My high school art teacher taught me this technique: don't draw every single branch. Be very, very light-handed with your brush, and barely drag it to make the lightest strokes possible. And, intersperse where the branches are visible between trees. What do I mean by this? Imagine the branch was broken into pieces, and that it was scattered on the floor. The branches wouldn't all connect at every juncture. If you paint the branches in a light, "broken" manner like that, then the appearance will make it look like the branches are intertwined, or layered in a real forest setting. Give it a try!

- If you look closely at the image above, you can see the "interspersed" branch style I'm talking about. When doing trees like this, I dab a light green in the background, then I come in with the darker colors and add some branch details.

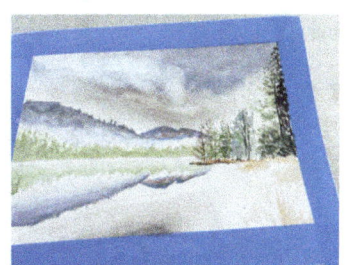

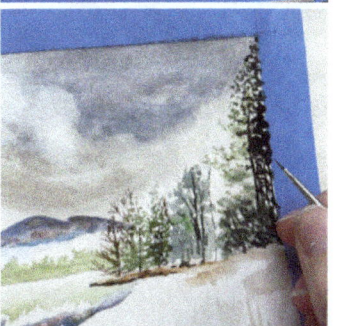

A Step-By-Step Watercolor Landscape Tutorial

Step 5: Paint the trees, from "trunk" then to "limb."

- Here's a closeup of the small brush I use. I also make a conscious effort to differentiate colors between the trees so that it is not an incomprehensible blob of the same shade of green. You can see here that Sap Green is mixed with Viridian, Ultramarine Blue, Burnt Sienna and Yellow Ochre.
- As you can see here, the darkest trees are the ones right in front. It gives the image depth.

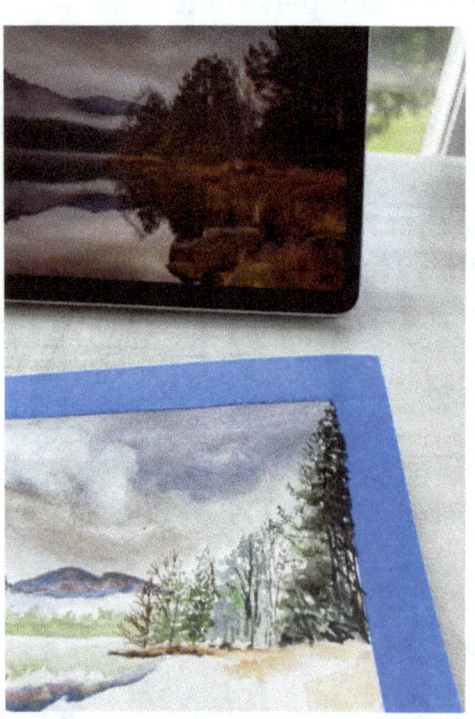
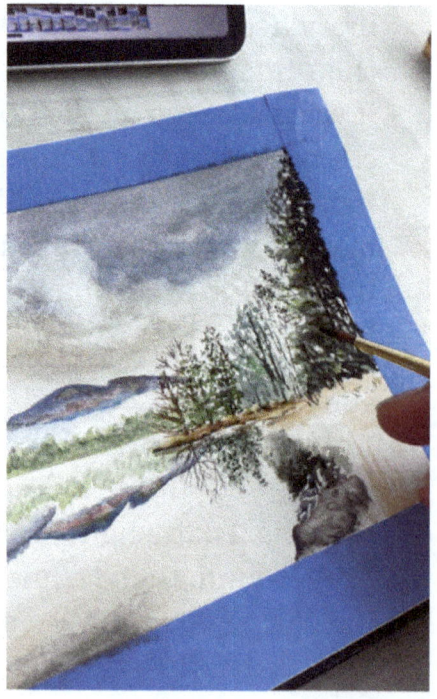

A Step-By-Step Watercolor Landscape Tutorial

Step 6: Paint the rocks, grasses, and shore.

- Once I have the trees finished, I fill in the grasses and rocks in the immediate foreground. For grasses, I paint from bottom to top: this creates a natural shape that mimics the thicker part of the grasses attached to the ground, and it gradually tapers upward.
- For rocks, I look at my image and see where the darkest shadows are. I create horizontal "hatch" marks that mimics the craggy, uneven surface of a rock. If you look at your photo, you'll see there are light spots, medium dark, and very dark spots; and without getting too exact, you can match these 3 value ranges.

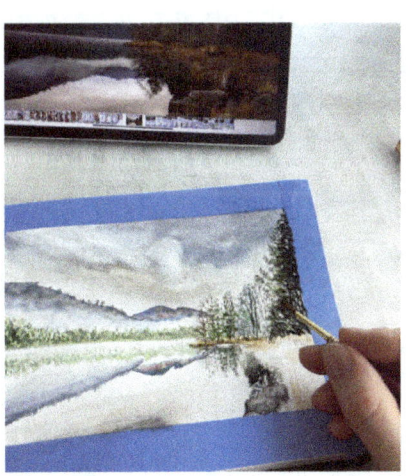
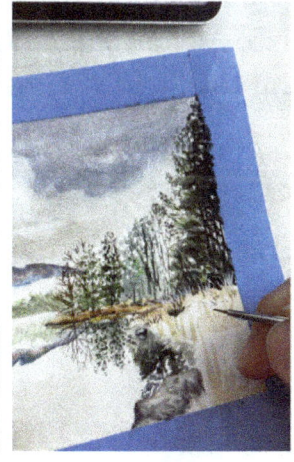

- Next I started painting the reflections of the trees and rocks in the water. These should be blurrier than the actual trees, but nice and dark to denote how close they are to the viewer.

A Step-By-Step Watercolor Landscape Tutorial

Step 7: Finishing touches.

- Usually I go back in and finish up the sky and lake, or any big areas that weren't quite finished during the first pass. In this case, I painted more cloud shapes in the sky.
- Then I take my small brushes and do any finishing touches. I added darker grasses and shadows on the shore, and finished the color gradient on the mountain in the middle of the page. When I don't see any more details to add or I feel like I'm finished, then I sit back and peel the tape!
- And you're done! I hope this step-by-step tutorial was helpful for you. This was the exact process I used for this piece, and I believe it took me probably 4 hours from start to finish. Although, I will be honest, I'm not very good at keeping track of my time! Thanks again for visiting

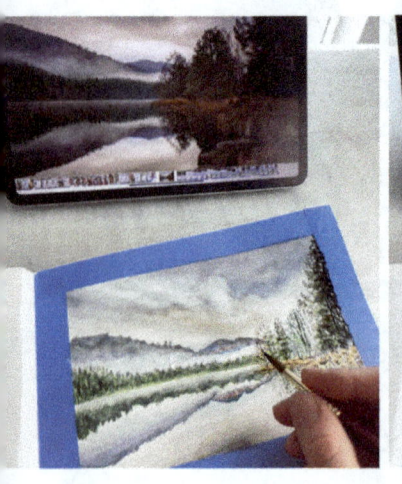
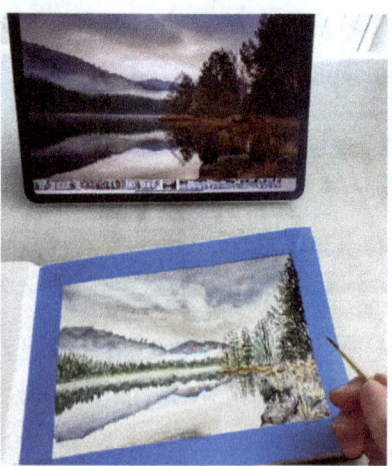
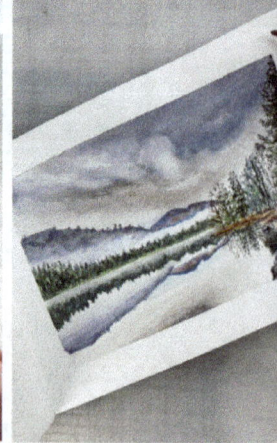

Lovely Loose Watercolor Flowers Tutorial

Supplies:

- A jar or tub of water
- Watercolor paints (Anything works; I am using a Crayola set that was less than $4. Also note that styrofoam egg cartons make awesome palettes.)
- Watercolor paper (I prefer 140 lb. 9" x 12" pads. The thicker the paper, the less likely it is to warp.) Note: blank watercolor cards are also great for this project.
- Brushes (My favorites are sizes 0, 2, and 6 round brushes)
- Paper towel to soak up excess water and paint
- Paper cutter (optional)

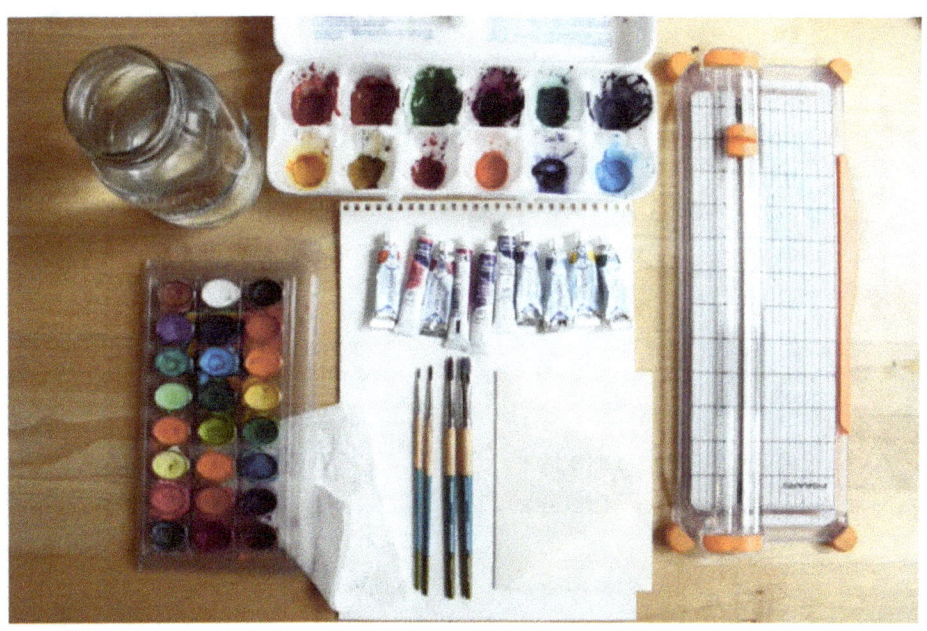

Lovely Loose Watercolor Flowers Tutorial

1. Cut the Paper

- First, cut your paper into the sizes you want to work with. I cut mine into 6" by 8" pieces to fold into 6" x 4" greeting cards. (The 9" x 12" watercolor pad makes two cards per page with some scraps leftover that I turn into bookmarks.)

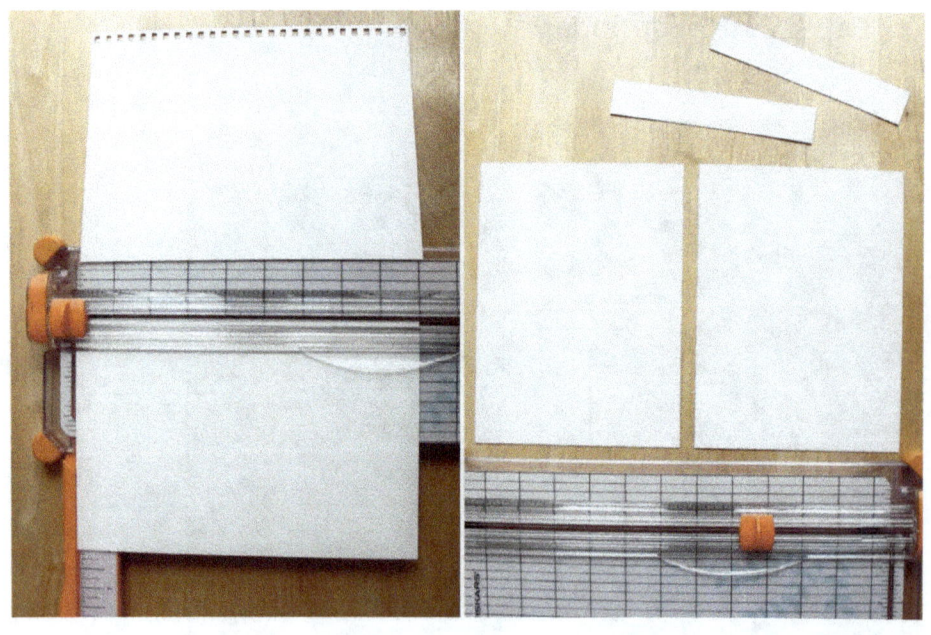

Lovely Loose Watercolor Flowers Tutorial

2. Choose Your Colors

- Next, choose the colors you want to use to paint your loose watercolor flowers. For this tutorial, I'm going to use yellow-green, dark purple, pink, magenta, and dark blue. You can use whatever colors you want, but I recommend choosing 2-4 shades that are next to each other on the color wheel for the flowers, and any shade of green for the leaves and the stems.

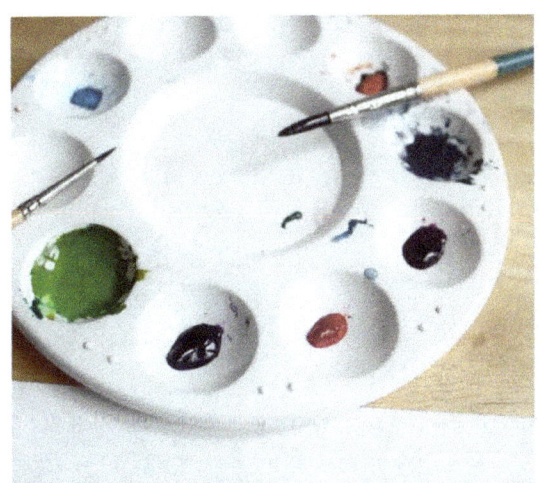

THE COLOR WHEEL

3. Paint a Poppy

- Let's start by painting a poppy-esque flower. Dip a medium size round brush into water, pick up some dark blue paint, and start by painting a "U" shape (1). Then, fill in the "U" shape so it looks like a side view of petals, and then paint a thinner squiggly shape above the lower petals. Be sure to leave a very thin white space between what is now the front and the back petals of the flower (2).

Lovely Loose Watercolor Flowers Tutorial
3. Paint a Poppy

- Before your first flower has a chance to dry, quickly clean your brush in water and saturate it with purple paint. Dab the purple along the bottom of the flower, and allow it to bleed into the blue for a shaded effect (3). If the color comes on too dark, you can blot it with a paper towel. Then, using your smallest brush, pick up some green paint and add a blob of green to the bottom of the flower. Let the paint bleed into the petals if it's still wet. In a delicate, quick motion, draw a line down from the flower for the stem (4).

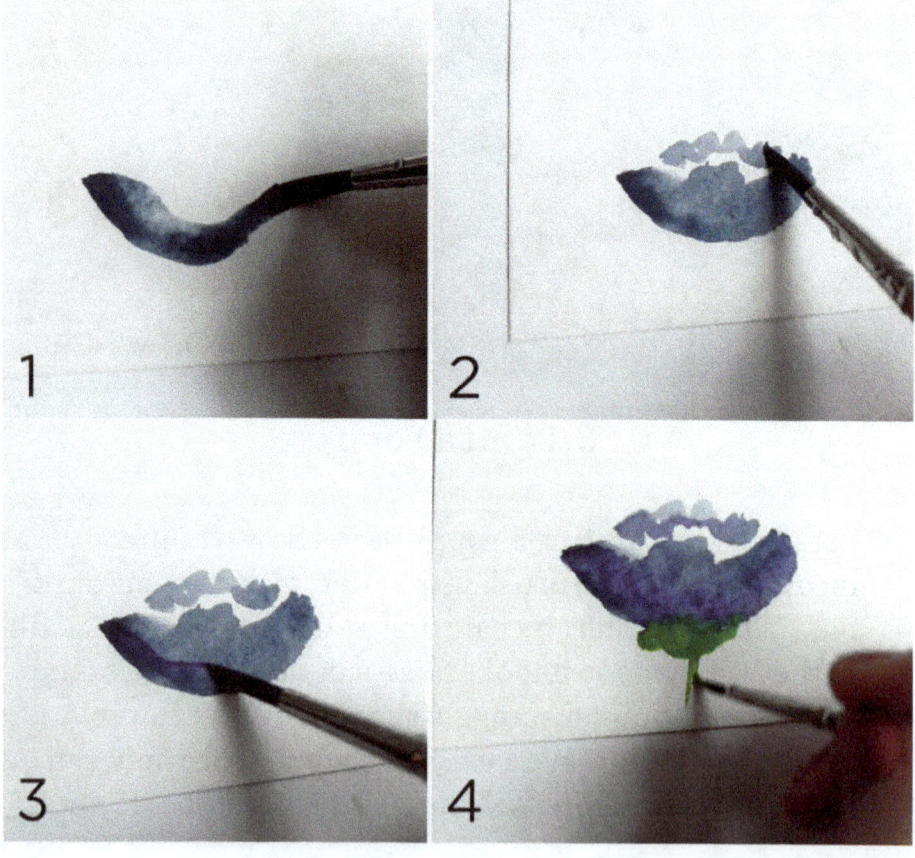

Lovely Loose Watercolor Flowers Tutorial
4. Paint a Thistle

- Now, let's make a flower that looks like a thistle. I'm using magenta paint and my size 0 brush. Quickly swipe the paint down in curved lines from one central point in an umbrella shape (1). Pick up more water and paint as your brush dries out. Then use green paint to add a curved stem to the flower, again using a very quick and light sweep of the smallest brush (2).

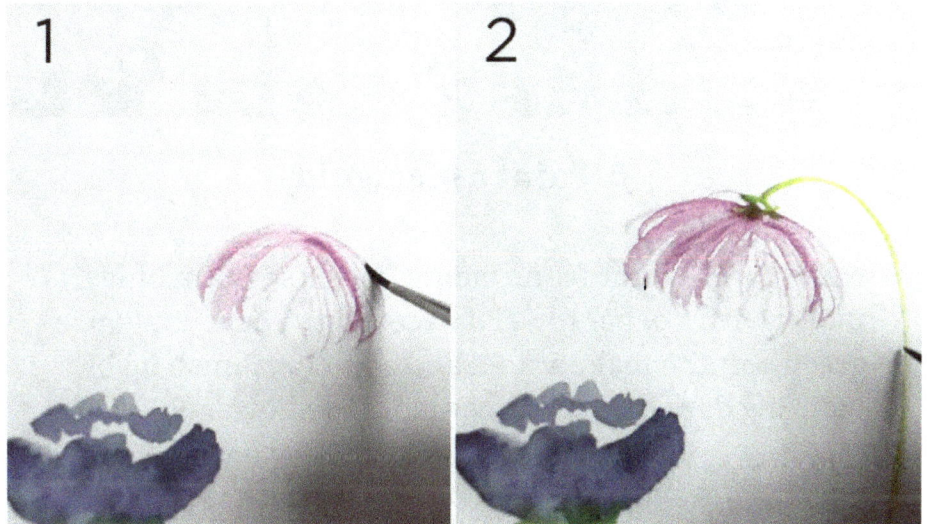

5. Paint a Flower Bud

- Now, let's have a Bob Ross moment and make a happy little flower bud. Draw a curving stem, and then use blue paint to make a little blob at the end of the stem (1). Use purple paint to add a dot of contrasting purple to the bud (2).

Lovely Loose Watercolor Flowers Tutorial

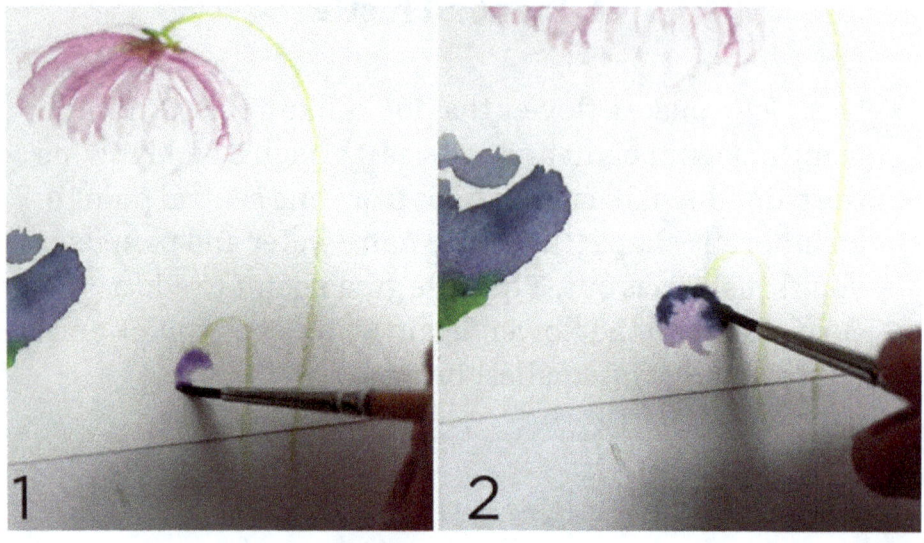

6. Paint a Marigold

- Now, paint a basic front-facing flower shape in blue (1). Blot it with a paper towel if necessary. Then, use your green paint to make a stem and a leaf (2). Finish up by painting dark dots in the center of the flower (3).

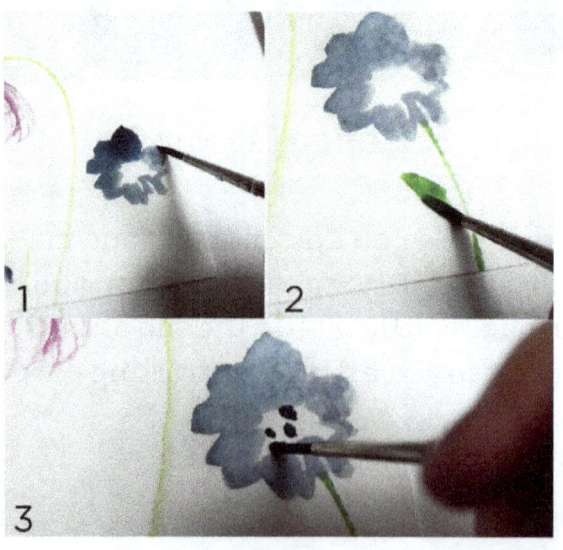

Lovely Loose Watercolor Flowers Tutorial

7. Paint Another Poppy

- Now, paint another poppy flower in blue and purple, using a similar technique as the very first flower. Feel free to make it a slightly different shape!

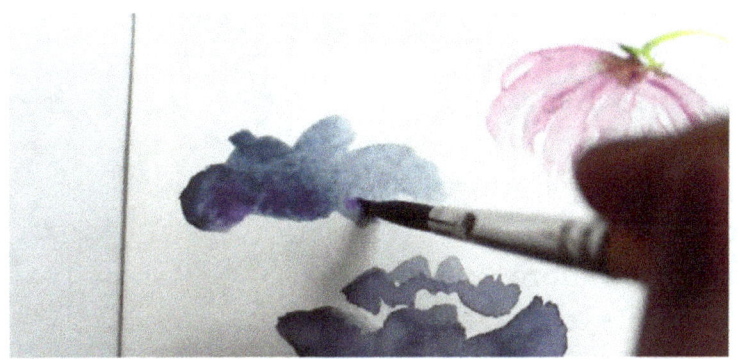

8. Add More Details

- Once you've painted your flowers, feel free to go through and add more details. My first poppy needed a little more contrast (1), and my thistle was looking a little sparse, so I went back and filled it in with some more color (2).

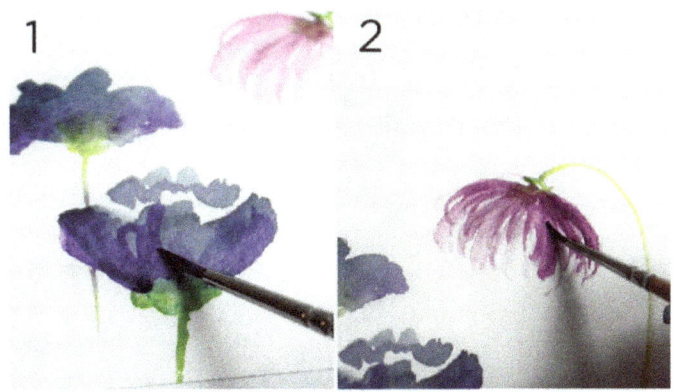

Lovely Loose Watercolor Flowers Tutorial

9. Enjoy — and Paint More Florals!

- Once the paint dries, you can fold your watercolor paper in half and admire your gorgeous watercolor card! If you're enjoying the painting process, go on to create a few more cards while you have the momentum.

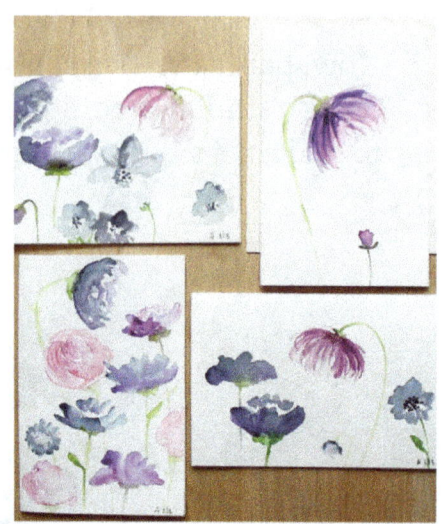

Extra Credit

- To paint roses or peonies, make "C" shapes out from a central point with a small brush, making the "C's" bigger as you extend out from the center.
- And there you have it! I hope I've inspired you to pick up a brush and try some watercolor painting. It's very relaxing and fun!

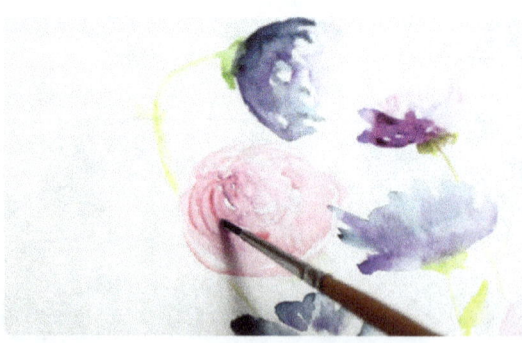

THANK YOU FOR READING!

www.ingramcontent.com/pod-product-compliance
Lightning Source LLC
Chambersburg PA
CBHW070350230526
45471CB00006B/2508